The Jury System

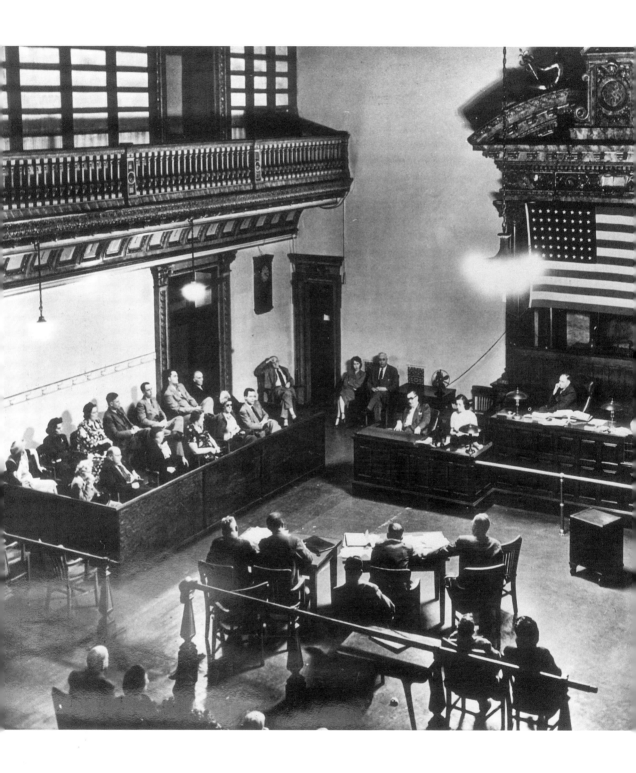

CRIME, JUSTICE, AND PUNISHMENT

The Jury System

Robert V. Wolf

Austin Sarat, GENERAL EDITOR

CHELSEA HOUSE PUBLISHERS
Philadelphia

Chelsea House Publishers

Editor in Chief Stephen Reginald
Managing Editor James D. Gallagher
Production Manager Pamela Loos
Art Director Sara Davis
Picture Editor Judy Hasday
Senior Production Editor Lisa Chippendale

Staff for THE JURY SYSTEM

Senior Editor John Ziff
Associate Art Director/Designer Takeshi Takahashi
Picture Researcher Gillian Speeth
Cover Illustration Janet Hamlin

First Printing

1 3 5 7 9 8 6 4 2

Library of Congress Cataloging-in-Publication Data

Wolf, Robert V.
The jury system / Robert V. Wolf; Austin Sarat, general
editor.
   p. cm. — (Crime, justice, and punishment)
Includes bibliographical references and index.
Summary: Traces the history of the jury system in the
United States and discusses the modern process with
emphasis on such topics as deliberation and verdicts and
proposals for reform.

ISBN 0-7910-4599-4 (hardcover)

1. Jury—United States—Juvenile literature. [1. Jury.]
I. Sarat, Austin. II. Title. III. Series.
KF8972.Z9W65 1997
347.73'752—dc21   97-37320
                                                             CIP
                                                             AC

Contents

CRIME, JUSTICE, AND PUNISHMENT

CAPITAL PUNISHMENT

CLASSIC CONS AND SWINDLES

DETECTIVES, PRIVATE EYES,
AND BOUNTY HUNTERS

THE FBI'S MOST WANTED

HATE CRIMES

INFAMOUS TRIALS

THE JURY

JUVENILE CRIME

PRISONS

RACE AND CRIME

REVENGE AND RETRIBUTION

RIGHTS OF THE ACCUSED

SERIAL MURDER

TERRORISM

VICTIMS AND VICTIMS' RIGHTS

WHITE-COLLAR CRIME

Fears and Fascinations:

An Introduction to Crime, Justice, and Punishment

By Austin Sarat

We live with crime and images of crime all around us. Crime evokes in most of us a deep aversion, a feeling of profound vulnerability, but it also evokes an equally deep fascination. Today, in major American cities the fear of crime is a major fact of life, some would say a disproportionate response to the realities of crime. Yet the fear of crime is real, palpable in the quickened steps and furtive glances of people walking down darkened streets. At the same time, we eagerly follow crime stories on television and in movies. We watch with a "who done it" curiosity, eager to see the illicit deed done, the investigation undertaken, the miscreant brought to justice and given his just deserts. On the streets the presence of crime is a reminder of our own vulnerability and the precariousness of our taken-for-granted rights and freedoms. On television and in the movies the crime story gives us a chance to probe our own darker motives, to ask "Is there a criminal within?" as well as to feel the collective satisfaction of seeing justice done.

Fear and fascination, these two poles of our engagement with crime, are, of course, only part of the story. Crime is, after all, a major social and legal problem, not just an issue of our individual psychology. Politicians today use our fear of, and fascination with, crime for political advantage. How we respond to crime, as well as to the political uses of the crime issue, tells us a lot about who we are as a people as well as what we value and what we tolerate. Is our response compassionate or severe? Do we seek to understand or to punish, to enact an angry vengeance or to rehabilitate and welcome the criminal back into our midst? The CRIME, JUSTICE, AND PUNISHMENT series is designed to explore these themes, to ask why we are fearful and fascinated, to probe the meanings and motivations of crimes and criminals and of our responses to them, and, finally, to ask what we can learn about ourselves and the society in which we live by examining our responses to crime.

Crime is always a challenge to the prevailing normative order and a test of the values and commitments of law-abiding people. It is sometimes a Raskolnikov-like act of defiance, an assertion of the unwillingness of some to live according to the rules of conduct laid out by organized society. In this sense, crime marks the limits of the law and reminds us of law's all-too-regular failures. Yet sometimes there is more desperation than defiance in criminal acts; sometimes they signal a deep pathology or need in the criminal. To confront crime is thus also to come face-to-face with the reality of social difference, of class privilege and extreme deprivation, of race and racism, of children neglected, abandoned, or abused whose response is to enact on others what they have experienced themselves. And occasionally crime, or what is labeled a criminal act, represents a call for justice, an appeal to a higher moral order against the inadequacies of existing law.

Figuring out the meaning of crime and the motivations of criminals and whether crime arises from defiance, desperation, or the appeal for justice is never an easy task. The motivations and meanings of crime are as varied as are the persons who engage in criminal conduct. They are as mysterious as any of the mysteries of the human soul. Yet the desire to know the secrets of crime and the criminal is a strong one, for in that knowledge may lie one step on the road to protection, if not an assurance of one's own personal safety. Nonetheless, as strong as that desire may be, there is no available technology that can allow us to know the whys of crime with much confidence, let alone a scientific certainty. We can, however, capture something about crime by studying the defiance, desperation, and quest for justice that may be associated with it. Books in the CRIME, JUSTICE, AND PUNISHMENT series will take up that challenge. They tell stories of crime and criminals, some famous, most not, some glamorous and exciting, most mundane and commonplace.

This series will, in addition, take a sober look at American criminal justice, at the procedures through which we investigate crimes and identify criminals, at the institutions in which innocence or guilt is determined. In these procedures and institutions we confront the thrill of the chase as well as the challenge of protecting the rights of those who defy our laws. It is through the efficiency and dedication of law enforcement that we might capture the criminal; it is in the rare instances of their corruption or brutality that we feel perhaps our deepest betrayal. Police, prosecutors, defense lawyers, judges, and jurors administer criminal justice and in their daily actions give substance to the guarantees of the Bill of Rights. What is an adversarial system of justice? How does it work? Why do we have it? Books in the CRIME, JUSTICE, AND PUNISHMENT series will examine the thrill of the chase as we seek to capture the criminal. They will also reveal the drama and majesty of the criminal trial as well as the day-to-day reality of a criminal justice system in which trials are the exception and negotiated pleas of guilty are the rule.

When the trial is over or the plea has been entered, when we have separated the innocent from the guilty, the moment of punishment has arrived. The injunction to punish the guilty, to respond to pain inflicted by inflicting pain, is as old as civilization itself. "An eye for an eye and a tooth for a tooth" is a biblical reminder that punishment must measure pain for pain. But our response to the criminal must be better than and different from the crime itself. The biblical admonition, along with the constitutional prohibition of "cruel and unusual punishment," signals that we seek to punish justly and to be just not only in the determination of who can and should be punished, but in how we punish as well. But neither reminder tells us what to do with the wrongdoer. Do we rape the rapist, or burn the home of the arsonist? Surely justice and decency say no. But, if not, then how can and should we punish? In a world in which punishment is neither identical to the crime nor an automatic response to it, choices must be made and we must make them. Books in the CRIME, JUSTICE, AND PUNISHMENT series will examine those choices and the practices, and politics, of punishment. How do we punish and why do we punish as we do? What can we learn about the rationality and appropriateness of today's responses to crime by examining our past and its responses? What works? Is there, and can there be, a just measure of pain?

CRIME, JUSTICE, AND PUNISHMENT brings together books on some of the great themes of human social life. The books in this series capture our fear and fascination with crime and examine our responses to it. They remind us of the deadly seriousness of these subjects. They bring together themes in law, literature, and popular culture to challenge us to think again, to think anew, about subjects that go to the heart of who we are and how we can and will live together.

*   *   *   *   *

Perhaps no part of the American legal system is as fascinating and perplexing as the jury system. Juries give citizens a substantial role as decision makers in legal trials, and, as such, they democratize law and express respect for the capacities of ordinary men and women to deal responsibly with weighty matters. In so doing, jury service has the potential to provide a distinctive form of civic education, as Alexis de Tocqueville said, to "rub off that private selfishness which is the rust of society." The juror, in Tocqueville's opinion, was taught as a result of his service to "judge his neighbor as he would himself be judged." Yet today such optimism about the jury seems quite out of date. Today doubts about the motivations and capacities of jurors, about their willingness to pay heed to evidence and do what the law asks of them, abound. Americans no longer have unquestioned confidence in the wisdom of the jury system.

It is against this background that *The Jury System* should be read. How did we move from optimism to pessimism, from the high-mindedness of Tocqueville's view to post–O. J. Simpson doubts? By providing a wonderful history of the jury and a careful look inside the jury room, this book helps provide an answer. Along the way it reminds us of the power that juries wield and of the potential both for good and for abuse that goes with that power. This book explores the way juries epitomize a complex intersection between democracy and law even as it explores worrisome trends. It illuminates the disparate pulls that every juror and every jury faces and provides a gripping look at the difficult decisions that citizens must make when they are called to jury service. *The Jury System* is invaluable not only in raising important questions about juries, but also in pointing the way toward humane and effective responses.

THE
JURY SYSTEM

I n the United States, a power that once rested in the hands of kings now rests with an extraordinary group of ordinary people. That group is called a jury, and they are charged with the most crucial job in a courtroom: deciding where truth lies and determining which side wins.

What makes them so extraordinary? For one thing, members of a jury are strangers to one another, brought together for a brief time by the call of civic duty. They might occupy vastly different socioeconomic strata and have widely varying levels of education, but in the jury box the corporate executive sits beside the day laborer, and the college professor rubs elbows with the high school dropout. They might have different skin colors, along with the different life experiences that implies.

Arena of justice: When 12 ordinary citizens take the seats at right, they become arbiters in a struggle involving conflicting versions of the truth. At stake can be millions of dollars or even life or death.

They are young and old, liberal and conservative, male and female. And yet, despite their varied backgrounds, their often conflicting worldviews, and their unfamiliarity with one another, they are almost always able to reach agreement—and not just agreement by a majority, but unanimous agreement, a remarkable feat in our pluralistic society.

In the American legal system, each of the major actors—law enforcement, attorneys, judge, and jury—plays a well-defined role. All except the jury are justice system professionals, and to a great extent, the jury's role is circumscribed by the decisions of these professionals in specific cases as well as by the rules governing the overall functioning of the legal system. In the first place, most cases are disposed of before the jury's involvement would be necessary. And when a jury does hear a case, its role is largely passive: the attorneys argue the case with the judge acting as a kind of referee, and strict rules of evidence limit what the jurors are permitted to know. Within these limited parameters, however, the jury wields substantial power: the right to pass judgment on another human being; the authority to decide between imprisonment and freedom, sometimes even life and death; and the power to move potentially vast sums of money from one party to another, in reparation for harm done.

At one time, only monarchs or dictators had such power, but in our democracy, that power is given to ordinary citizens. Thomas Jefferson saw it as an essential ingredient of our freedoms, writing, "Were I called upon to decide whether the people had best be omitted in the Legislative or Judiciary department, I would say it is better to leave them out of the Legislature. The execution of the laws is more important than the making of them."

When a person becomes a juror, the normal routines of his or her life stop. Jurors are asked to drop their jobs and other responsibilities for a limited time to

Thomas Jefferson, author of the Declaration of Independence, third president of the United States, and a strong proponent of the jury system.

grapple with the responsibility of deciding a case. They are plunged into a world of someone else's conflicts and problems. If it's a criminal case, for instance, the jurors might be asked to decide whether someone is a murderer or a petty thief. In a civil case, they are asked to decide whether a wrong was done and, if so, to place a value on the harm caused—whether to an individual, a group, or even an entire community.

Why is this group of strangers, who have no special qualifications for the task, entrusted with such an important job? Although most people would agree that the jury system itself is far from perfect, for centuries it has been widely felt that allowing ordinary citizens to decide matters of justice is the best way to guarantee that criminals and victims alike are treated fairly. A nation's sense of right and wrong, after all, comes from the collective values of its citizens; and a jury is, in a way, an attempt to create a mini-nation, or a mini-community, that applies its common values to the case at hand.

Of course, common values are not always an ideal measuring stick because they can also reflect a community's prejudice and ignorance. In the past, all-white juries, particularly in the South, were known to convict black defendants accused of crimes against whites on the flimsiest of evidence and, conversely, to acquit white defendants accused of crimes against blacks despite solid cases against them. Jurors have also been known to judge the players in a trial by their looks, their mannerisms, or other irrelevant factors. Some jurors have taken bribes. Some have fallen asleep during key testimony.

And yet, despite some experts' criticisms of certain aspects of the jury system and despite occasional public furor over a controversial verdict, in most cases a majority of Americans seem satisfied with the job juries do in sending the guilty to their punishment and compensating the wrongfully injured—or, at least, cases in which they express disapproval of a verdict are relatively rare. The belief, perhaps, is that somehow the jury will collectively overcome the deficiencies of its individual members, that in the end reason will overcome passion, and common sense triumph over ignorance. As a famous attorney, Marvin Belli, once pointed out, "When the jury returns its verdict, right or wrong, one seeing this picture is at once satisfied with the result; yet he would not be tried by any one of these twelve individually."

This book takes a look at the history of the jury system, examines the system as it exists today, and guides the reader through the various stages in the life of a jury, from the selection of jurors through the trial, the deliberations, the verdict, and beyond. The final chapter examines some criticisms of the jury system and describes proposals that have been put forth to improve it.

Although the jury stands as an enduring symbol of America's democratic ideals—a cross section of ordinary citizens assembled without prejudice to see that justice is done—the institution we have today is actually the product of centuries of development in various cultures. And the American jury system continues to evolve under the mandate of Supreme Court decisions and pressures from various groups to reform.

EARLY JURIES

The idea of the jury system came from the same society that invented democracy itself: the ancient Greeks. That was well over 2,000 years ago, and their notion of a jury was quite different from what we have today. Still, the Greeks were the ones who first came up with the idea of giving average citizens the power to issue verdicts at trials.

The Greek system relied on *dikasteries*, groups of 6,000 randomly selected citizens over 30 years old. This large group was then divided into groups of 200 to 500 men (since women weren't citizens, they couldn't serve on juries). These smaller groups were called *decuries*, and their members were known as *dikasts*. When a trial came up, a *decury* was selected by lot to hear the case. Because they were so large, *decuries* were virtually immune to bribery, but their size also made them difficult to manage. Each *dikast* received a meager payment for his work, a reimbursement so small that usually only the poor were willing to participate. Historians doubt

From a time before juries, lawsuits, and divorce attorneys: A domestic dispute is "tried" in medieval Europe, with the winner of the fight being declared the winner in the case. As a handicap, the husband must fight from a hole, whereas the wife may move freely anywhere in the circle of stones.

that the *decuries* were always fair in their verdicts. For instance, one jury historian asserts that many wealthy people were found guilty merely because the *dikasts*, who were poor, resented those who had more money.

The Romans, who were deeply influenced by Greek culture, borrowed the jury system from Greece. A Roman juror, known in Latin as a *judix*, was a private citizen selected to decide a case. It's not known today how *judices* (the plural of *judix*) were chosen, but objections could be made if a juror was deemed to be prejudiced. In A.D. 352, however, the Roman emperor Constantius II, believing that juries had acquired too much power, abolished them.

Ancient Athens, the birthplace of democracy, was also the birthplace of the jury system. Below: Greeks, at left, explain their system to Roman legal scholars. Opposite page: Athenian jurors' tickets, made of clay. The holes were made to keep score of the arguments.

But the concept of juries wouldn't go away. More than 500 years later, Scandinavian cultures continued the jury legacy. In Norway a system was developed in which 36 people were chosen to serve as a jury. Unless their decision was unanimous, however, a legal expert appointed to oversee the jury could overturn it. And the opinion of the legal expert could, in turn, be overruled by the king. Sweden had 12-person juries on which agreement among only 7 members was necessary for a verdict. Denmark used 24-person juries, and Iceland had juries made up of members of the aristocracy. The Scandinavians brought the idea of the jury system to Normandy around the year 890, and William the Conqueror carried the concept

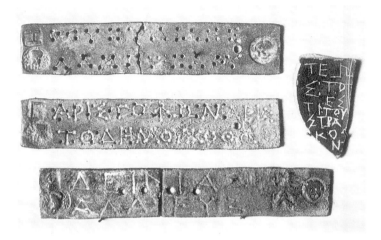

from Normandy to England when he invaded in 1066.

It is the English system from which the modern American jury system directly evolved. But you would hardly recognize today's jury in the methods employed in England nearly a thousand years ago.

Before William the Conqueror arrived, trials in England were settled in a number of ways. One of the most common methods was compurgation. If it was a civil case, both sides brought with them their friends, called compurgators. Usually at least 12 friends were required. The compurgators swore that their associate was honest and that his cause was just. The person with the most compurgators won. In one case, it has been reported that a man seeking title to a piece of property showed up at trial with a thousand compurgators.

In criminal cases, the rules were essentially the same. As long as the defendant wasn't caught in the act and had sufficient compurgators to swear to his innocence, he was acquitted. The defendant might be found not credible, however, if he'd been previously accused of a crime or if he didn't bring enough friends to testify on his behalf. In such a case, the defendant was forced to undergo the ordeal.

For an average citizen, this meant either having his head or arm placed in boiling water (if the water didn't harm him, he was deemed innocent) or having his thumbs tied to his toes and being tossed into a body of water (if he sank, he was found innocent; if he floated, he was judged guilty). The ordeal for nobility was equally brutal. First, the defendant's hand was sprinkled with holy water. Then, a red-hot iron, weighing from one to three pounds, was placed on his hand and he had to take nine paces, after which he threw down the iron, ran to the altar, and had his hand bound. The bandages came off after three days, and if the hand had healed, he was deemed innocent.

William the Conqueror brought with him his own ways of administering justice, some of which were no less barbaric than those already being used in England. Under Norman law, opposing parties often literally fought it out, either battling each other one-on-one or hiring others to represent them in physical combat.

But the Normans also brought with them tribunals—usually made up of 16 people—that drew up accusations. The tribunals, called *assizes,* consisted of representatives of different neighboring localities. They were gathered together by the sheriff at the request of the royal justices. The appearance of the justices in a particular town signaled an *eyre,* as the traveling court was called. When the justices arrived, they told the tribunals what matters, such as all felonies, they were required to report. Each tribunal, whose members were essentially jurors, gave the justices their *veredicta*—a list of people whom they accused of committing the crimes.

Cases were handled in various ways. In some cases, the tribunals reported the felony; in others, they reported that an "appeal," or private prosecution, had been made. A felony accusation could be tried immediately if the members of the tribunal had named a defendant and the defendant was present, or it could go directly to a condemnation if a confession had been made to local officials or if guilt was in some other way obvious. Generally, the accused denied the charge, or the assize

Although 16-person tribunals—a rudimentary jury—existed in England by the end of the 11th century, their job was merely to report people accused of certain crimes to the royal justices. Guilt or innocence was established by various "physical proofs." Here an accused woman undergoes the ordeal by walking barefoot over red-hot ploughshares.

could name the accused, as was their duty, but then say that they didn't really suspect him. In general, the assize did not judge the guilt or innocence of the accused, however. Their job was merely to make the accusation. Guilt or innocence was still usually determined by ordeal or through compurgation. Nonetheless, by drawing together representative citizens to consider criminal misdeeds, the Normans, under Henry II in 1166, established a tradition that today lives on in the functioning of a grand jury.

A private prosecution, as mentioned above, consisted of an accusation made by the victim against the supposed perpetrator. One way the accused could fight such an accusation was to claim that the charge had been made out of spite. He could then buy a writ to have a jury consider the issue. Even though the jury was technically considering only whether the appeal had been made from hate or spite (as opposed to just cause), it was essentially considering guilt or innocence as well. If the jury found the accusation had arisen from hate or spite, the appellee, as the accused was called, was off the hook; but if the jury found otherwise, then the accused had to submit to physical proof, which meant either combat between the appellor (the accuser) and appellee or an ordeal.

In 1215 the Catholic Church banned the ordeal, which led to a transformation in the way justice was administered. Suddenly, prisons began springing up. They were used to house those accused of committing serious crimes and against whom there was solid evidence or strong suspicion of guilt. Those accused of crimes of medium gravity were generally expelled from the country, while those accused of the least serious crimes were required to pledge that from now on they would conduct themselves responsibly.

Prisons began filling up—understandably, since the only sentence was a life term. The government responded by offering prisoners a choice: either spend the rest of your life in jail or submit to a trial by jury to determine your guilt or innocence.

Despite the truly horrifying conditions in medieval English prisons, many prisoners refused to submit to a jury trial, fearing the worst possible outcome of a guilty verdict—execution. That eventually led judges to require those accused of the most serious crimes, such as murder, to undergo trials by jury whether they wanted to or not.

These juries, however, were far different from the juries we have today. Perhaps the biggest difference is that while today jurors are expected to be impartial and know nothing about the alleged crime before the trial, back in the 13th and 14th centuries in England, jurors were selected precisely for what they knew about the circumstances of the alleged crime. Many of the jurors actually knew the accused personally and had firsthand knowledge of the facts of the case. Jurors were encouraged to use what they previously knew about the crime and, in particular, what they knew of the accused's character to reach a verdict.

As time went on, the institution evolved. The presenting jury, which made the accusations, and the trial jury, which decided guilt or innocence, became two separate entities. In addition, by the 15th century jurors were less likely to have firsthand knowledge of the facts of the case, and the presentation of the trial was handed over to the defendant's accusers and government authorities.

Although juries by this time had been given the incredible power to free men or send them to their death, their verdicts were not inviolable—they could be changed or reversed. Furthermore, it was not above the authorities to attempt to coerce a jury's decision, sometimes by locking jurors up without food or drink until they had reached a verdict. Even worse was something called *attaint*—literally, "a stain upon honor or purity." If authorities deemed a verdict improper, they could convene another jury that would convict the original jury of having brought disgrace to the process by issuing a wrong verdict. The original jurors then faced the possible loss of their liberty and the confiscation of their property.

THE EVOLUTION OF THE JURY

The power that the jury enjoys today was established in large part during one of the most famous trials in the history of the jury system. That trial, which occurred in London in 1670, involved two men, William Mead and William Penn. (After the trial, Penn emigrated to the American colonies and founded the commonwealth of Pennsylvania.)

Mead and Penn, both Quakers, stood charged with unlawful assembly for preaching their religion on the street. The two men didn't deny that they had broken the law; instead, they argued that they should be allowed to preach in public, regardless of the law. The

In this painting by American artist John Trumbull, Thomas Jefferson, flanked by the four other members of his committee, presents the Declaration of Independence to the Continental Congress. The document listed the colonists' major grievances against the king of England, among which was "depriving us in many cases, of the benefits of Trial by Jury."

judge in the trial specifically informed the jury that Mead and Penn had broken the law, and yet the jury refused to convict. This infuriated the judge, and he fined the jurors. Four jurors appealed the fine, resulting in a decision by the Court of Common Pleas, which found that jurors could not be fined or imprisoned for their verdicts. This was an incredible turning point in the history of the jury. It meant that jurors were now free to decide verdicts as they saw fit—they could even ignore the law in doing so, because now they had the power to acquit without risking punishment for an unpopular decision.

The English brought the jury system with them to the American colonies, although defendants were not granted jury trials in all cases. This eventually surfaced as an important complaint in the Declaration of Independence, whose signers listed among the king of England's offenses "depriving us in many cases, of the benefits of Trial by Jury" and "transporting us beyond Seas to be tried for pretended offences. . . ."

The role of juries was particularly important to the colonies because it was the only way for average citizens to have a say in the administration of justice. In fact, in the famous case of printer John Peter Zenger, a jury showed that it had the power to defy the authority of a king.

The case against Zenger, which was tried in 1735, involved a charge of seditious libel. A German immigrant, Zenger printed the *New-York Weekly Journal*, a paper whose pages were largely devoted to criticizing New York's royal governor, William Cosby. While nominally the *Weekly Journal*'s publisher, Zenger—whose command of English was limited—in fact exercised no editorial control. The articles, all of which were unsigned, were written and edited by Cosby's opponents.

When the *Weekly Journal* ran a series of articles lambasting Cosby for firing a judge who had ruled

The 1670 trial of William Mead and William Penn (pictured here) for unlawful assembly was a watershed in the history of the jury system. It established the principle that jurors couldn't be punished for rendering a verdict the state didn't like.

against him in a personal equity case, the authorities filed seditious libel charges against Zenger. Because seditious libel was defined as publishing something negative about "any public man whosoever for any conduct whatsoever, or upon any law or institution whatever," regardless of whether the story was true, the case seemed fairly straightforward. If it could be proved that Zenger had, in fact, published the negative articles, he would presumably have to be found guilty.

But Andrew Hamilton, Zenger's brilliant attorney, conceived a bold defense strategy: he admitted that his client had published the articles in question but declared that a publisher had the right to print stories "supported by truth," essentially challenging the prosecution to show where the falsehood lay in the paper's charges against Cosby. The prosecution wasn't about to be drawn into defending the governor's record—it couldn't, as what the *Weekly Journal* had printed was true—but under the law, the accuracy or inaccuracy of the newspaper stories was irrelevant.

The judge also rejected Hamilton's defense, informing the jury that the articles were libelous and instructing the jurors to decide only whether or not Zenger had published them—a moot point, since his attorney had already admitted he had. But Hamilton didn't give up. In an impassioned summation, he "urged the jury to disobey the instructions of the court and to determine for themselves whether the laws of England made it a crime to punish truthful criticism of government," as Jeffrey Abramson reports in his book *We, the Jury*. The jury chose to acquit, in defiance of the court and the king's wishes—just one of many defiant stands colonists took against England in the years before the Revolutionary War.

After the colonists won their freedom from England, they enshrined the right to a trial by jury in the Constitution. The right was considered so important as an antidote to tyranny that three amendments deal directly with jury guarantees. The Fifth Amendment deals in part with grand juries, saying, "No person shall be held to answer for a capital, or otherwise infamous crime, unless on a presentment or indictment of a Grand Jury, except in cases arising in the land or naval forces, or in the Militia, when in actual service in time of War or public danger. . . ."

The Sixth Amendment addresses criminal prosecutions, guaranteeing a speedy trial. It also addresses an issue that the former colonists felt was particularly important—that a defendant should not be tried far away from where he or she allegedly committed the crime, perhaps among hostile strangers, but in the place

ON THIS SITE
AUGUST 4, 1735
JOHN PETER ZENGER
WAS ACQUITTED OF CHARGES THAT HE
PUBLISHED LIBELOUS STATEMENTS ABOUT
THE ROYAL GOVERNOR OF NEW YORK.
THE JURY PROCLAIMED TRUTH TO BE A JUST
DEFENSE AGAINST CHARGES OF CRIMINAL LIBEL,
THEREBY ESTABLISHING THE CORNERSTONE
OF A FREE AMERICAN PRESS.

EMBEDDED AUGUST 4, 1958
BY
SIGMA DELTA CHI
NATIONAL PROFESSIONAL
JOURNALISTIC FRATERNITY

"EVERYONE WHO LOVES LIBERTY OUGHT TO ENCOURAGE FREEDOM OF SPEECH"

JOHN PETER ZENGER

where the crime occurred, in front of a jury drawn from that community. This notion harks back to the early days of juries in England, when jurors often personally knew the facts at hand. The strength in this, according to Patrick Henry, lay in the fact that the jurors were "neighbors . . . acquainted with [the defendants'] characters, their good or bad conduct in life." The Sixth Amendment therefore reads, in part: "In all criminal prosecutions, the accused shall enjoy the right to a speedy and public trial, by an impartial jury of the State and district wherein the crime shall have been committed. . . ."

The Seventh Amendment addresses civil suits: "In Suits at common law, where the value in controversy shall exceed 20 dollars, the right of trial by jury shall be preserved, and no fact tried by a jury, shall be otherwise

This plaque marks the site of printer John Peter Zenger's 1735 acquittal on charges of seditious libel. The case, a landmark in the history of freedom of the press, is also a prominent example of jury nullification: the jurors conspicuously disregarded the law in rendering their decision.

re-examined in any Court of the United States, than according to the rules of the common law."

These constitutional provisions apply, however, solely to federal courts. Only later, when the Fourteenth Amendment was adopted, were state jury trials addressed in the Constitution. The Fourteenth Amendment reads, in part, "[N]or shall any State deprive any person of life, liberty, or property, without due process of law. . . ." Due process has been interpreted to mean, among other things, the right to a jury trial in a state court. All the states, as they joined the Union, adopted constitutions that guaranteed the right to trial by jury, except for Louisiana, which put this guarantee into legislation.

A basic democratic principle underlies the jury system: that all citizens should have a voice in making important decisions rather than leaving that right in the hands of an individual or a privileged group. In the case of juries, ordinary citizens retain the right to settle disputes and decide who, as a result of a crime, will lose their liberty or life. References to an "impartial" jury and a "jury of one's peers" also reflect the democratic ideal. But in practice, the jury system has often fallen short of these lofty goals.

Until recently, African Americans were excluded from jury service regularly and blatantly, especially in the South. Even after the Supreme Court banned laws explicitly prohibiting blacks from serving on juries in 1880, prejudiced local officials still managed to exclude African Americans. All-white juries continued to be selected, even in counties whose populations were overwhelmingly black. The result was that prejudice often affected the verdicts, and black defendants were convicted at disproportionately higher rates than were white defendants. This was particularly true when a black defendant stood accused of committing an act of violence against a white victim. If the victim and the defendant were black, however, all-white juries were sometimes less likely to take the crime seriously, as if that was "what one expects from a negro," according to a University of Chicago study done in the 1950s.

Women also have been excluded from jury service. Historically, they were called to serve on juries only in special circumstances. In the colonies, for instance, a "jury of matrons" would be convened to determine whether a woman sentenced to die was pregnant (if the finding was affirmative, the execution was postponed until after she gave birth). But no jurisdiction permitted women to serve on regular trials until 1870. In that year, Wyoming Territory granted women the right to vote and hold public office, and some local courts in the territory also allowed women to sit on juries. The first time women served with men on a jury trial was probably in Laramie City, Wyoming Territory, in March of 1870. But there was an immediate backlash, and opponents of women jurors raised all sorts of arguments—for example, that women were too delicate to confront the gritty and often vulgar world of a criminal trial, that they were too emotional, or that their place was in the home. By September of 1871, women were no longer serving on Wyoming juries.

Women remained ineligible to serve on juries in every state until 1898, when Utah allowed them to be jurors. Slowly, other states followed suit: Washington in 1911, Kansas in 1912, Nevada in 1914, California in 1917, Michigan in 1918. After the 1920 passage of the Nineteenth Amendment, which guaranteed women the right to vote, more states opened the doors of the jury room to both sexes, but it wasn't until the 1940s that a majority of states had authorized women for jury service. And as recently as 1975, several states treated men and women differently: men were drafted into service on juries, whereas women had to volunteer if they wanted to serve.

Some states also tried to exclude daily-wage workers on the grounds that they couldn't afford to lose

These jurors heard the case of a man accused of murdering a police officer in 1925. Note that all are well-dressed white men of middle age or older. Until fairly recently, many American courts routinely excluded minorities, women, and even daily-wage workers from jury service.

money while serving on a jury. But the Supreme Court ruled in 1946 that poorer people cannot be excluded because the jury system would turn into "the instrument of the economically and socially privileged." Despite that ruling, the Court said it was acceptable, in a case the following year, to test people for intelligence and English comprehension—tests that, in effect, excluded large numbers of manual laborers who were not well educated.

On the federal level, and in many states as well, the method of selecting jurors favored the elite. The system used was called the "key-man" system. The so-called key men were citizens who had been selected for jury service by community leaders. These people themselves were generally community, civic, and business leaders, and they made up only a small portion of the society at large. They typically came from the same churches and community organizations, and they weren't representative of the entire local population. One study showed that in a midwestern town in the 1950s, virtually all jurors were Republicans, attended church, and were active in community service organizations—a very homogeneous group. This system was justified by the notion that the dispensing of justice required more integrity, intelligence, and morality than the average citizen could muster, but it also allowed community leaders covertly to exclude blacks and other minorities whom they viewed as undesirable.

In 1968 Congress abolished the blue-ribbon juries in federal courts, and in 1975 the Supreme Court applied the principle to state courts as well. The 1968 law, called the Jury Selection and Service Act, required that grand and petit (that is, trial) juries in the federal system be selected by random drawing. The ultimate goal was to end discrimination in the selection of juries—and not just because discrimination in itself was considered bad, but because discrimination affected the quality of justice that was dispensed. This relates to the relatively modern idea that the best juries are those that represent a cross section of the community. From a practical perspective, having a jury include a cross section of the community means that as many perspectives and insights as possible are brought to bear on the evidence.

A case illustrating the harm that can arise when a jury doesn't represent a wide range of views is the conviction of Han Tak Lee, a Korean-born man found guilty of murdering his daughter through arson in the Pennsylvania community of Stroudsburg. Some of the jurors who heard Han's case in 1990 said they were influenced by the defendant's lack of emotion as he was brought to the charred building where his daughter's body was found. No Asian Americans served on the jury, however, and Asian Americans later decried the verdict, saying that it's unusual for a Korean man to cry, and Han's lack of tears, instead of communicating guilt necessarily, merely reflected Korean custom.

Today, some people view cross-sectional juries critically, claiming that rather than bring an enlightened new perspective to a case, jurors representing different sexes, ethnic groups, and socioeconomic backgrounds simply bring their own prejudices to the table. Some said this was obvious in the two O. J. Simpson trials, in which the football Hall of Famer, who is black, was acquitted of the murders of two white victims—his former wife, Nicole Brown Simpson, and her friend Ronald Goldman—by a black-majority jury in a criminal trial, and yet found liable for the same crime in a civil trial heard by an almost all-white jury. The assumption of critics was that the jurors voted on the basis of allegiances wrought by skin color—the black jurors backing the black defendant and the white jurors sympathizing more with the white victims—even though the jurors in both trials denied this. Such thinking, in fact, challenges the integrity of the jury system, by assuming that jurors aren't pursuing the truth but are merely arguing from their own preconceived notions—almost, as writer Jeffrey Abramson puts it, "as if a juror had been sent by constituents to vote their preferred verdict."

In theory, the idea that juries should reflect the community's diversity also conflicts with the oft-repeated declaration that every defendant is entitled to a jury of his or her peers. Taken literally, this would require that jurors closely resemble the defendant in background and social position, as a peer is defined as one who belongs to the same societal group. Clearly, such a system would prove problematic. Could only rich people hear cases involving rich defendants, African Americans hear cases involving African Americans, and teenagers hear the cases of other teenagers? Or, taken a step further, would a woman charged with killing her abusive husband be entitled to a jury of other victims of domestic abuse?

In reality, resolving the tension between the dual values of entitlement to a jury of one's peers and creating juries that are representative of the community largely boils down to semantics. "Peer" can be defined merely as an equal. In a democratic society, all citizens are equals in the eyes of the law, so a jury of one's peers simply means a jury of one's fellow citizens. As the Supreme Court has interpreted this over the past few decades, all that is required is that the jury pool reflect the characteristics of the general geographic area in which the crime occurred.

THE
MODERN JURY

What is a jury? In dictionary terms, it is a group of people sworn to reach a verdict based on evidence in a matter presented to them.

Most Americans would probably add that a jury must include 12 people; that it must reach a unanimous verdict; that it must hear evidence from both sides of a case; that it has the power to decide only questions of fact and not of law; and that it reaches its decision only after a great deal of thoughtful deliberation.

But these statements are only sometimes true. There are, in fact, many exceptions to these principles and many different ways in which a jury functions.

In this scene from the 1957 motion picture 12 Angry Men, *actor Henry Fonda, playing the lone holdout on a jury that wants to convict, forcefully makes a point. The film presented the jury system as we'd like it to work, with reason overcoming passion as jurors undertake a methodical examination of the evidence in their search for truth. The reality is often quite different.*

To Prospective Juror:

You have been selected at random as a Prospective Juror to serve in the Court of Common Pleas of Philadelphia. If you are qualified, you may be subpoenaed to serve for one day or one trial.

In accordance with the Act of Legislature, you are requested to fill out this qualification form and return it in the enclosed envelope within ten (10) days from receipt hereof.

YOU ARE CAUTIONED THAT FAILURE TO RETURN FORM PROPERLY AND TRUTHFULLY ANSWERED WILL SUBJECT YOU TO A FINE OR IMPRISONMENT OR BOTH. ANY FALSE ANSWER WILL SUBJECT YOU TO THE PENALTY OF PERJURY. These questions are necessary to determine your qualifications to serve as a juror. Your answers are treated as Confidential. If you are unable to fill out this form, have another person do it for you and indicate the reason for the assistance.

Detach this stub and return card in enclosed envelope

	QUESTIONNAIRE FOR PROSPECTIVE JUROR
Date of Birth: _____/_____/_____ *(Month, Day, Year)*	
Home Phone: _____ Business Phone: _____	NUMBER
Have you ever been convicted of a crime punishable by imprisonment for more than one year? ☐ Yes ☐ No	☐ MR.
Can you read, write and understand the English language? ☐ Yes ☐ No	☐ MRS **SAMPLE**
Are you physically and mentally able to serve as a juror? ☐ Yes ☐ No	☐ MISS
Are you a U.S. citizen? ☐ Yes ☐ No	☐ MS.
	PLEASE INDICATE ANY CORRECTIONS TO NAME & ADDRESS BELOW:
REMARKS *(Use space below to complete any answers on questionnaire which require more information or more space.)*	
_____	I hereby certify that the above answers are true and correct
_____	
_____	_____
	(Sign Your Name) *(Date)*

30-31 (Rev. 9/96)

Courts conduct much of the preliminary work of finding jurors by mail. Above: A jury questionnaire, designed to screen out potential jurors who may not be suitable for hearing a case. Opposite page: A jury summons, which tells a citizen where and when he or she is to report for actual jury service.

The classic 1957 film *12 Angry Men* has helped enshrine as a national myth the notion of 12 people struggling with the evidence in a search for truth. In the film, Henry Fonda plays the lone juror pressing for acquittal in a murder case. The camera never leaves the jury room as he slowly but methodically convinces every last juror to change his initial vote of guilty. It's a tremendous display of thought over passion, of reason over prejudice.

But juries in real life can be quite different. First of all, it would be highly unlikely to have an all-male jury now that women are eligible for service. Also, juries are now required to draw from a cross section of society, which, in many communities, means that an all-white jury like the one in the film is a rarity. In addition, since the making of the film, the Supreme Court has found that the 12-person jury is a historical artifact and not constitutionally required, and many states now allow

SUMMONS TO REPORT FOR JURY SERVICE
JURY SELECTION COMMISSION
CRIMINAL JUSTICE CENTER
1301 FILBERT STREET
PHILADELPHIA, PA 19107

By Order of the **Honorable Alex Bonavitacola**, President Judge, Court of Common Pleas, you are summoned to appear for Jury Service in **ROOM 101, 1301 FILBERT STREET**, on the time and date shown below.
FAILURE TO OBEY THIS SUMMONS IS PUNISHABLE BY FINE AND/OR IMPRISONMENT

MICHAEL J. McALLISTER, ESQ.
JURY COMMISSIONER

SAMPLE

DATE TO REPORT	TIME

IDENT NO.: _____

BRING THIS SUMMONS WHEN YOU REPORT

(OVER)

30-343 (Rev. 9/96)

PLEASE READ THESE INSTRUCTIONS CAREFULLY   (SAMPLE)

LENGTH OF JURY SERVICE
The Court of Common Pleas of Philadelphia County has instituted a term of jury service whereby jurors selected to sit on a trial panel will serve only for the duration of that one trial. Those who are not chosen for a particular trial will complete their service at the end of the day on which they report.

SUMMONS
If necessary, your summons should be shown to your employer PRIOR to your service date so as to indicate that you have been summoned to serve. BE SURE TO BRING YOUR SUMMONS WHEN YOU REPORT FOR JURY DUTY. Certification for your employer will be attached to your jury fee check which you will receive at the end of your jury service.

POSTPONEMENTS
If there is grave illness in your family or other serious problem which would constitute an undue hardship or extreme inconvenience for you to appear in court on the date specified and would require an alternate date, you must notify the Jury Commissioner in writing at least 10 days prior to your service date.
TELEPHONE CALLS ARE NOT ACCEPTABLE

PLEASE RETURN THIS SUMMONS WITH ANY CORRESPONDENCE TO:
JURY SELECTION COMMISSIONER
CRIMINAL JUSTICE CENTER
1301 FILBERT STREET, ROOM 204
PHILADELPHIA, PA 19107

OR FAX YOUR SUMMONS AND CORRESPONDENCE TO:
(215) 683-7183

WHERE AND WHEN TO REPORT
REPORT TO THE JURY ASSEMBLY ROOM #101 on the date and time indicated on your summons. It is suggested that you use public transportation, since the City is not responsible for car or parking fees. Please bring a pen or pencil.

ATTIRE
Please use good judgment and come properly dressed when you report for jury duty. Remember, you are performing a most important civic duty; please dress accordingly. Shorts and tank tops are not acceptable.

JURY SERVICE—A VITAL FUNCTION OF DEMOCRACY
Jury Service is one of the highest duties of citizenship. It is also a very interesting experience and will give you an opportunity to learn more about our system of justice and how it works. While it may require some adjustments of your normal schedule to serve as a juror, we hope that under the One Trial/One Day jury system, any inconvenience will be minimal and that you will enjoy the opportunity to see your courts in action and to participate in this vital democratic process.

Weapons and cellular phones
are not permitted in the building.

---

juries with as few as 6 people in both civil and minor criminal matters. The Court has also decided that unanimity is not always required, and many states now allow for nonunanimous verdicts, although usually only in civil cases.

Juries today are randomly selected from public rolls, such as tax rolls, driver's license data banks, and voter registration listings. Prospective jurors are notified by mail that they must report for jury service at a particular time and place, although noncompliance with such requests is very high. The national no-show rate has been estimated at 55 percent. Prospective jurors are warned that noncompliance can translate into a contempt-of-court citation, but those who fail to show up are rarely punished.

Prospective jurors must sometimes return to a courthouse waiting room day after day while they wait to be selected for service on an actual jury, and sometimes, even after days of waiting, they aren't picked. In Massachusetts in 1988, for instance, the state courts summoned 905,795 potential jurors. Ultimately, 314,436 were scheduled to appear (the rest obtained postponements or exemptions), and only 253,436 actually did appear. Of those, 118,277 were sent to a courtroom and only 38,797 were impaneled (selected for a jury).

To make this waiting time less inconvenient, many states have adopted what is known as a one-day/one-jury rule, which means that prospective jurors are required to wait only one day to see if they're chosen for service, and, if they are chosen, need serve on only one jury. Some jurisdictions allow jurors to call up in the morning to find out if they'll be needed that day; if not, they don't have to show up at the courthouse.

While actual service on a jury can often be fun and interesting, it is the time spent outside the courtroom that many prospective jurors dread. "Jurors are often treated like annoying interlopers," writes Stephen J. Adler in his book *The Jury: Trial and Error in the American Courtroom*.

> They wait in shabby, crowded assembly rooms, frequently staffed by hostile or condescending clerks. They are supposed to follow directions, ask no questions, make no demands. When they move from room to room, they go as a group, escorted by men in uniform. Many jurors complain that they feel as if they are on trial, that they are not there to judge but to be judged.

One form of jury that generally gets little public attention is the grand jury, a group that meets secretly

to hear evidence presented by a prosecutor. Unlike criminal and civil trials, which are conducted publicly and which allow the defense to present evidence and examine witnesses, a grand jury investigation focuses only on the prosecution's side of the case, and a person being investigated doesn't even have the right to be present during the proceedings. The size of grand juries varies from state to state. In New York, for example, grand juries are composed of 23 persons, with a quorum of 16 being necessary to conduct business. If 12 grand jurors, a majority, believe that the person being investigated probably committed a crime, the grand jury will file an indictment. An indictment is an accusatory document—not a finding that the person *is* guilty—setting forth the charges against the defendant and compelling him or her to answer those charges in court.

Prospective jurors file into a courthouse in New York. Jury service involves waiting, standing in lines, and, frequently, being dismissed abruptly and without explanation. Many people consider jury service boring and inconvenient, and, according to national estimates, more than half of the citizens summoned fail to appear.

Some states require that a grand jury first issue an indictment in order for a felony prosecution to take place. Other states use grand jury indictments in some felony cases but also allow prosecutors to submit written statements that outline their reasons for believing the accused has committed a crime. And more than a dozen states have outlawed grand juries entirely, giving prosecutors alone the power to decide whether or not to file charges against a defendant. In the federal courts, the Fifth Amendment requires that before someone can be tried for "a capital or otherwise infamous crime," a grand jury must issue an indictment.

If a grand jury votes to indict, the defendant is brought to an arraignment, at which he or she pleads either guilty or not guilty. If the defendant pleads guilty, the next step is sentencing. But if the defendant pleads not guilty, a trial date is set. Often the actual trial can begin only after pretrial hearings. At such hearings, the defense usually challenges the admissibility of the prosecution's evidence—for instance, a defense attorney might claim that a confession was coerced. Once the judge decides which evidence is admissible and which is not, the trial is set to begin. The jury is then selected in a sometimes lengthy process. Following that, the actual evidence and witnesses are presented. Then, after closing arguments and the judge's instructions, the jury deliberates. A trial can last less than a day or many months, depending on the complexity of the case.

Civil trials are conducted somewhat differently. There is no grand jury; instead, one party brings a lawsuit against another. Typically, the party being accused of wrongdoing charges that the suit is meritless and asks a judge to dismiss it. If the judge disagrees, however, the trial moves forward. Both sides then conduct discovery, during which they share information and take depositions, which are pretrial interviews of possible witnesses and other key players. The purpose of such interviews is to gather information and evidence, which can help both sides map their strategy and assess the scope of the potential damage award. Once the trial is set to begin, the format is similar to that of a criminal trial, starting with jury selection, followed by the presentation of evidence and witnesses, and ending with the jury's deliberations.

No exact figure is available for the number of jury trials conducted annually in the United States, but one recent estimate, including both civil and criminal cases, puts the number at about 150,000. This reflects only a small number of cases handled by the justice system, however. An increasing number of cases are settled long before a trial begins. In criminal cases, this is done most often through something called a plea bargain, by which the prosecution offers a reduced charge and sentence in exchange for a guilty plea by a defendant. In civil cases as well, the mere threat of a trial often pushes both sides to reach what is known as an out-of-court settlement.

In the 1940s, about 15 percent of felony prosecutions reached a jury trial, while today less than 5 percent of such cases do, according to a recent estimate. In federal court in 1990, about 11.5 percent of criminal prosecutions and only 2 percent of civil cases went to jury trials. Cost is perhaps the main reason for this trend. Faced with an ever-increasing number of cases to handle, prosecutors simply don't have the time or the resources to take every accused criminal to trial, so they're often willing to accept a plea bargain. And in civil cases, aside from the high costs of protracted litigation, the parties risk losing big if their case is decided by a jury, so an out-of-court settlement for a lesser sum often makes an attractive option.

CHOOSING
A JURY

You're led into a wood-paneled courtroom by a uniformed bailiff who directs you to sit in a hard, uncomfortable chair. The judge, cloaked in a long, black robe, stares down at you from the bench. There are several attorneys in the room as well. They're all dressed in dark business suits. Though they offer a friendly smile, you can see that they're examining you carefully. In a short while, the judge and the attorneys start asking you questions: What do you do for a living? Where do you live? What television shows do you watch? What newspapers do you read? Have you ever been the victim of a crime? Are there any police officers in your family? Have you ever known anyone who was raped? What do you think of immi-

This courtroom sketch depicts the first day of jury selection in the trial of four men accused of the 1993 World Trade Center bombing. The process of questioning jurors to uncover potential biases can be arduous and time-consuming in high-profile cases such as this one.

grants? Would you have trouble believing the testimony of an 11-year-old child?

Some of the questions are easy to answer; some, not so easy. It's almost as if you're on the witness stand, maybe even as if you're the person who has been accused of a crime—after all, why else would these representatives of the legal system be grilling you so intently, the way police interrogators might question a crime suspect? But, in fact, you're not a suspect, and you're not on trial. You are actually a member of the jury pool—a prospective, or potential, juror. And the questions you're being asked are intended to elicit a simple but important piece of information: Can you be fair and unbiased in assessing the evidence that will be presented to you during the upcoming trial?

This process of questioning prospective jurors is known as the voir dire, a phrase borrowed from the French, which means "to speak the truth." It is the method by which a jury, usually of 12 people, is selected from the much larger jury pool. At its most basic, the voir dire is intended to weed out prospective jurors who may have already made up their minds about the case and those who, because of prior knowledge, past experience, or personal belief, might be predisposed to favor one side over the other. Ideally, a jury would be composed of people who have no opinions and no knowledge of the case.

It cannot be expected, of course, that jurors have absolutely no opinions about anything. That would be impossible. In a trial involving a horrific chain of serial killings, for instance, how could an average juror not be repulsed by a description of the crimes? What is hoped, however, is that the juror won't jump to the conclusion that the person accused of the crimes is guilty because the juror has heard reports on the evening news that seem to indicate that the defendant committed the crimes or because the juror doesn't like the defendant's skin color, or religion, or the fact that

the defendant lacks a college education, or has a foreign accent. In other words, the ideal juror will consider only the evidence presented at trial and won't be swayed by personal prejudice when reaching a verdict.

In most trials, a jury can be impaneled in a couple of hours or less. Usually, a jury of 12, plus 2 alternates, can be found by putting about 50 prospective jurors through the voir dire process. In only the most high-profile cases, when it's hard to find a juror who hasn't heard about a case, do hundreds of prospective jurors have to be questioned.

In some states, the attorneys write their questions down and the judge does all the asking. In other states, the attorneys themselves quiz the prospective jurors directly. The questions asked vary from trial to trial. If a police officer will be testifying at the trial, for example, it's common to ask whether prospective jurors have any police officers in their families or know any cops personally (such connections might indicate an unfair

Defense attorney Robert Shapiro speaks to the press before the beginning of O. J. Simpson's murder trial in 1995. Shapiro described jury selection in the case as "a war of nerves, like an ultimate chess game" between the defense and prosecution.

bias in favor of the police). Prospective jurors would also be asked whether they have ever had a run-in with the police (indicating a possible bias against cops). The concern here is that someone who unduly favors the police might give the testimony of the officer too much weight, while a person who dislikes cops might swing in the other direction, discounting the officer's testimony even if all signs indicate that the officer is speaking truthfully.

Answering yes to questions such as "Is there a police officer in your family?" or "Have you ever been arrested?" doesn't mean that a person is automatically excluded from the panel. In some communities, it might be almost impossible to find jurors without strong feelings about the police. So the judge will then ask the juror whether, despite personal connection or experience, he or she can suspend any preconceptions and judge a police officer's testimony fairly. Most people in such a circumstance say they can be open-minded. Some experts maintain that personal opinions will affect a juror's judgment anyway, whether the juror realizes it or not. There's no way to tell, of course, if a particular juror is truly capable of being open-minded, but in most cases the judge simply takes the prospective juror's word for it.

The truth is, it's simply human nature to have preconceived notions and opinions. The best that jurors can do, therefore, is try to be open-minded. And the attorneys for both sides know this. That's why their

Draped in an Israeli flag, the coffin of Rabbi Meir Kahane, a radical Jewish leader, is carried by mourners. Attorney William Kunstler (opposite page) won an acquittal for his client, an Arab named El Sayyid A. Nosair accused in the fatal shooting of Kahane, despite the fact that Nosair was caught running from the crime scene moments after the shooting with the murder weapon in his hand. The attorney attributed this stunning trial victory to his success in selecting "third-world people" as jurors. Others saw it simply as a bad verdict.

main interest isn't really eliminating bias entirely from the jury pool, but trying to find jurors whose outlook and attitudes will make them sympathetic to their side of the case. California defense attorney Robert Shapiro, in describing the voir dire process preceding the trial of his most famous client, O. J. Simpson, made precisely this point. "[B]oth sides," Shapiro wrote, "continued to say, of course, that they wanted a fair and impartial jury. In actuality, one side wanted a convicting jury, the other an acquitting jury."

Certainly, everyone agrees that those with obvious prejudice should not sit on a jury. For instance, a woman who has been raped cannot be expected to be impartial during a rape trial; nor can a member of the Ku Klux Klan be expected to fairly judge a case involving a black defendant.

But more subtle forms of bias are harder to detect, and these are the forms that attorneys, through probing questions and careful observation, hope to unearth and take advantage of. Many attorneys, in fact, consider jury selection an art, one on which the entire case depends. Shapiro described jury selection in the Simpson trial as a "war of nerves, like an ultimate chess game" between the defense and the prosecution. The outcome of that game resulted "in what I believe to be the most important aspect of any case: Who will judge the evidence," Shapiro said.

Attorneys often credit trial victories to the decisions they made during jury selection. When attorney William M. Kunstler won a surprise verdict acquitting his client El Sayyid A. Nosair of shooting and killing Rabbi Meir Kahane, a radical supporter of Israel and an anti-Arab leader, at close range in a Manhattan hotel in 1991, Kunstler said his effort to shape the jury panel was his most critical move. He said he sought a jury of "third-world people" and "people who were not yuppies or establishment types." Kunstler and his cocounsels were able to eliminate jurors who supported Israel and

those who might harbor biases against Arabs like Nosair. The jurors that remained were therefore more open to Kunstler's claim that Nosair was a victim of an anti-Arab conspiracy—even though Kunstler called no witnesses to back up that claim. Still, the jurors were so responsive to the defense's case that they apparently discounted undisputed evidence that Nosair was caught running from the scene with the murder weapon in his hand.

This example illustrates the tendency of many lawyers to stereotype prospective jurors. These stereotypes describe the expected behavior of certain groups of people—in the above case, Kunstler believed that supporters of Israel would have been more likely to convict Nosair than "third-world types." This belief, of course, had no basis in scientific fact, but was based merely on Kunstler's hunches and instincts, honed dur-

The murder trial of O. J. Simpson spawned a host of legal celebrities, but the woman conferring with the defendant in this photo, jury consultant Jo-Ellen Dimitrius, isn't one of them. Nevertheless, many observers regard the behind-the-scenes role of Simpson's jury experts as crucial in his acquittal.

A scene from the treason trial of Aaron Burr. Chief Justice John Marshall permitted the impanelment of jurors who had read about the highly publicized case, as long as the impressions they had formed would "yield to the testimony." Today familiarity with a particular case is generally a grounds for excluding a potential juror.

ing a long career of representing unpopular defendants. These kinds of hunches—distilled from the experience of countless attorneys—have found their way into jury-selection manuals, which over many decades have made claims like "Female juries are better for young, handsome male defendants, while male juries are better for female defendants."

One of the most famous defense attorneys of all time, Clarence Darrow, who represented "thrill-killers"

Nathan Leopold and Richard Loeb in 1924 and teacher John Scopes a year later at the so-called Monkey Trial, used to say that the Irish are "always the best jurymen for the defense" and that Scandinavians tend to favor the prosecution because they have "too strong a respect for the law as law." Much more recently, F. Lee Bailey, a defense attorney whose famous clients have included newspaper heiress Patty Hearst and O. J. Simpson, claimed that "heavy, round-faced jovial-looking persons" make the best defense jurors, while "the undesirable juror is quite often the slight, underweight and delicate type." Other similar stereotypes are described by writer Norman Sheresky in his 1977 book *On Trial: Masters of the Courtroom*:

> Prosecutors, for example, tend to excuse Jews—too emotional and sympathetic, they say. Personal-injury lawyers tend to excuse accountants, statisticians, employees of large companies and employees of all utilities. These people, the theory goes, are only comfortable with facts that can be put down on a piece of paper. They are uninclined and, frequently, unwilling (as opposed to artists, salesmen and performers) to translate human suffering and pain into dollars. A lawyer trying a matrimonial case in which the "guilt" he wishes to prove was adultery or cruel and inhuman treatment would want to excuse from the jury the more mature women, Catholics, Chinese and other staid groups. These people, he fears, would tend to feel, We stuck it out, why can't this plaintiff? Often, when there are two or three prospective women jurors and one is exceptionally good-looking, the first lawyer to question the prospective panel might excuse the attractive woman, almost immediately and brusquely, in the hope and expectation that the others will say to themselves, He is not taken in by her.

The approach described above may seem almost funny in its attempt to pigeonhole a person because of his of her religion, ethnic background, or profession. If, after all, every Jew or accountant thought the same way, then two Jews would never disagree about anything, and neither would two accountants. And what if a prospective juror was a Jewish accountant? Would the emotional side do battle with the rational side—and which side would win? Most attorneys today would agree that such questions are impossible to answer. But rather than give up on pigeonholing jurors, they've become even more diligent in trying to anticipate how a prospective juror would vote.

This diligence is reflected in a new business that has sprung up in the last 20 years called scientific jury selection. Its practitioners claim that through scientific means they can help a client select a jury that will have a strong inclination to decide a case in his or her favor.

Jury consultants charge huge sums of money, and only the most well-heeled of clients can afford them—although, on occasion, some jury-selection experts work for free on behalf of poor defendants. In 1994 it was estimated that 250 jury consultants were plying their trade in the United States and charging millions of dollars annually in consulting fees.

Jury-selection experts have played a role in many high-profile cases over the last decade, including the Simpson trial (during which both the prosecution and defense employed jury consultants). The most basic tool of the trade is the public opinion poll, by which the jury consultant—armed with information from the attorneys on how they intend to present their case—interviews hundreds of people in the community to create a profile of the ideal juror. The consultant presents this profile to the client before voir dire, facilitating the selection of jurors who will be most receptive to the client's case. Some consultants also advise clients *during* the voir dire process, by, for example, studying the prospective jurors' body language, including their posture, vocal tones, and eye contact. Other consultants favor handwriting analysis.

Although jury consultants claim that their work is a science, others scoff at the notion that a jury's sociological makeup can predetermine the verdict. "If scientific jury selection actually works, then facts and evidence play a subordinate role in trials," writes Jeffrey Abramson in his 1994 book *We, the Jury*. Abramson ridicules the notion that hidden social forces predispose different groups in the population to react to the same evidence differently. He feels that you can't pin down something as elusive as what a juror will think in a given situation—a juror may doze off during crucial testimony or misunderstand the judge's instruction, or some other unpredictable thing may happen at trial. While it's true that jury-selection experts can't guarantee a favorable outcome for their clients, lawyers evidently believe these consultants can provide an important advantage, for they're willing to spend substantial sums for consultants' services.

The voir dire itself in most cases is conducted orally—the judge or the attorneys simply ask prospective jurors questions. The attorneys usually exercise great care in how they present themselves during the voir dire. This is, after all, their first chance to make a favorable impression on the jury. A defense attorney will sometimes try to "humanize" his client by introducing him or her to the prospective jurors. An attorney might also try to establish a relationship with jurors by talking personally about himself or herself during the voir dire.

When a case has received a lot of pretrial publicity, the selection process can be incredibly arduous. In the so-called Preppy Murder Trial in which Robert Chambers was accused of killing Jennifer Levin in Central Park during a sexual encounter, it took two months in 1988 to select 12 jurors to hear the case. In the O. J. Simpson criminal trial, prospective jurors were given a 79-page questionnaire containing 250 questions, 12 of which focused specifically on comprehension of the science of DNA; it took five weeks before 12 jurors and 15 alternates were selected.

Although attorneys on either side of a case have the right to eliminate any number of jurors "for cause"—

that is, when a prospective juror can be shown to have some potential bias or prejudice in the case—more essential to a lawyer's ability to shape the composition of a jury are peremptory challenges. Peremptory challenges allow the attorney to eliminate a prospective juror for no particular reason; the attorney might simply have a hunch that the juror won't be sympathetic to his or her case. Both sides are usually granted, at the judge's discretion, from 3 to 15 peremptory challenges.

In the past, the right to peremptory challenges has often been abused. For example, in cases involving a black defendant, a prosecutor might have tried to eliminate blacks from the jury by using peremptory challenges.

In several landmark cases since 1986, however, the Supreme Court has banned the use of peremptory challenges if the purpose is to eliminate persons of a particular race or sex from the jury. Some have applauded these rulings as a step toward making juries more representative of the population at large. But attorneys have found ways to get around the Supreme Court's restrictions: they simply must advance a nonracial or non-gender-based explanation for striking undesirable jurors. A prosecutor recently was able to strike all Latinos from a jury in which the defendant was also Latino by claiming that it wasn't the jurors' ethnicity he objected to but the fact that they were bilingual. The prosecutor explained that since the defendant spoke only Spanish, the jurors were likely to interpret his words themselves rather than rely exclusively on the court-approved translation, as required by law. The Supreme Court ultimately upheld this rationale for dismissing all the Latino jurors.

In capital cases in which the jury will be called upon to decide the defendant's sentence if he or she is found guilty, prosecutors are allowed to assemble a "death-qualified jury." Such a jury consists of people who say they are willing to impose the death penalty, as opposed to jurors who are morally opposed to capital punishment and say they could not impose such a sentence regardless of the circumstances. In these cases, the prosecution uses the voir dire to eliminate the jurors who are opposed to the death penalty. Studies have shown, however, that this practice, which is condoned by the Supreme Court, tends to eliminate more women than men and more blacks than whites. At least one study shows that about 25 percent of the population is thus eliminated from the jury pool. Some say the end result is a jury that no longer represents a true cross section of the community; in fact, critics of the death-qualified jury charge, such juries are often more supportive of the police and more likely to convict than the community in general.

One of the most difficult obstacles to finding unbiased jurors is pretrial publicity. Though the problem occurs relatively rarely, when the news media have closely covered each twist and turn of an intriguing case, a large number of potential jurors may have, for example, seen or read about the arrest of the suspect and may know about some of the evidence against him or her. As previously discussed, in the old English jury system jurors with firsthand knowledge of the case were considered desirable. But in the early days of the United States, a new ideal began to emerge. That ideal was highlighted during the trial of Aaron Burr in 1807.

Burr, a former vice president, had been charged with treason for supposedly planning to seize New Orleans with a group of armed men. A huge amount of publicity had surrounded the incident, and when it came time to select a jury, most prospective members admitted to having read about the case in the newspapers. The question was, should anyone with an opinion about the case be struck from the jury, or should only those who had already made up their mind that Burr was guilty be prevented from participating? Chief Justice John Marshall, who presided over the trial, determined that merely having read the newspaper wasn't grounds for disqualifying a prospective juror, so long as the person had formed only "light impressions" of the case that would "yield to the testimony," as opposed to "strong and deep impressions which will close the mind against the testimony." Today, most judges no longer make the distinction between light and strong impressions. Instead, they try to exclude from the jury anyone who has read or heard anything about a case. Sometimes, however, that's impossible.

In the O. J. Simpson criminal trial, Judge Lance Ito tried to eliminate prospective jurors who regularly kept abreast of the news through newspapers, magazines, or television. This was an incredibly hard thing to do, however. At one point during the jury-selection process, the prosecution claimed that Simpson's name had turned up in 15,310 newspaper articles. To combat the massive amount of publicity the case was receiving, Ito forbade any member of the jury pool from having any contact with the news whatsoever. This meant, as Robert Shapiro describes it, that "one juror was eliminated for watching a cartoon with her children, one for turning on a Spanish soap opera, one for waking up to a clock radio, and one for walking into a bar that had a television on."

Perhaps the most famous example of pretrial publicity involves Jack Ruby, who, at 11:17 A.M. on November 24, 1963, shot and killed Lee Harvey Oswald, the accused assassin of President John F. Kennedy. As the manacled Oswald, flanked by police detectives, was being led out of the Homicide Bureau of the Dallas Police Department to be transported to a county jail, Ruby pushed through a crowd of journalists, thrust a pistol into Oswald's side, and fired. Millions of Americans saw the entire episode live on national television, and linked as it was to the assassination of the president, the murder became one of the biggest news events of the century. The incident was

replayed countless times over the airwaves in Dallas and around the country.

As a result of the avalanche of publicity, Ruby's attorney, Marvin Belli, claimed it would be impossible for his client to get a fair trial in Dallas. He asked that the trial be held in another jurisdiction (in legal terms, moving the trial to another location is known as a change of venue), but the request was denied. (The Court of Criminal Appeals in Texas later found that

The ultimate in pretrial publicity: Jack Ruby shoots Lee Harvey Oswald, the accused assassin of President John F. Kennedy. The killing was captured live on national TV.

the refusal to grant the change of venue was an error, and Ruby was awaiting a retrial when he died in prison in 1967.)

Belli also insisted that the Code of Criminal Procedure of Texas forbade the seating of any juror who had seen the shooting on television if counsel objected. He argued that by watching the shooting on TV, a prospective juror essentially became a witness in the case and thus could no longer be considered impartial. The defense lawyer was overruled, however, and 11 of the 12 jurors selected to hear the case admitted they'd seen the shooting on television. In a footnote to a 1976 decision, the Supreme Court expressed doubt that, because of the nationwide publicity around Ruby's case, an impartial jury could have been found anywhere in the United States.

This leads to another important issue regarding jury selection. Some observers say that the effort to eliminate from juries anyone who has heard anything about a particular case eliminates—especially in high-profile cases—the better-educated, more civic-minded, and generally more enlightened people from the jury pool. That's because those are the citizens who read papers, listen to the radio, watch TV news, and generally take an interest in community affairs. But aren't those people precisely the kind of citizens we'd want to have participate in our criminal justice system, critics ask? When they're excluded, the jury is "dumbed down." And not only does this corrupt the ideal of the jury—that its members be drawn from a cross section of society—but practical issues of competency may also arise. Are jurors who eschew even the most minimal effort to stay abreast of current events likely to be capable of sifting through the facts of a complex case? Aren't we left, critics wonder, with a jury of *ignorant* peers rather than a genuine cross section of the community?

These criticisms aside, in truth a jury is rarely a cross section of the community, whether or not the case has received abundant publicity. The Supreme Court has required only that the pool from which jurors are drawn be a cross section of the community at large. When it comes to picking the actual jury, attorneys on both sides, empowered by their right to make peremptory challenges, have wide discretion to shape the panel to their liking.

THE TRIAL

A jury means different things to different people. To a defendant in a criminal trial, the members of the jury are the most important people in the world—they have the power to grant the defendant freedom or, in the most serious cases, condemn him or her to death. To the defense and prosecuting attorneys, the jurors are a professional challenge—a group to be charmed, impressed, and persuaded, as though the members of the jury were judges scoring an Olympic event. To the judge, the jurors are honored guests who must be treated according to a set of rules as complex as any etiquette handbook. The judge must not only ensure that the jurors' needs for food and other comforts are met, but must also restrict the jury's access to information to that which the law deems admissible in court—all in the

Appealing to the jury, Hollywood style. From the 1941 courtroom drama The Trial of Mary Dugan.

Prosecutor Christopher Darden directs the jury's attention to a chart during the Simpson murder trial. Effective lawyers not only communicate their case clearly and forcefully, they also connect with jurors on a personal level.

interest of conducting a fair trial.

In the vast majority of criminal cases the jury's job is only to determine the facts of a case (except in Indiana and Maryland, where jurors are also given the power to determine the law as well). However, in capital cases many states give juries an awesome additional responsibility: deciding whether the defendant, if convicted, will receive life imprisonment or a death sentence. Questions of fact in a criminal case might include: Did the defendant have the opportunity to commit the crime? Does physical evidence link him or her to the crime scene? If a weapon was used, did he or she have access to it? Does the defendant have a believable alibi? Ultimately, does the evidence prove, beyond a reasonable doubt, the defendant's guilt? In a civil trial the facts might be more mundane, but nonetheless it is the facts with which the jury is supposed to concern itself: Did the defendant sign a contract with the plaintiff? Was the contract valid? Did the defendant break the contract? Answers to these questions are called findings of fact, and, in theory, these findings lead the jury to a verdict of guilty or not guilty—or, in a civil trial, a verdict of liable or not liable.

But from the very outset of a trial, much more than facts comes into play. The attorneys on both sides of a case know that the evidence might be just one of the factors that sways the mind of a juror, and so they do whatever they can to cajole, charm, bully, or tweak the members of the jury into their camp. Chances are, the lawyers began to court the jurors during voir dire. The defense attorney might have put her arm around her client's shoulder to underscore the defendant's humanity, for example, or the prosecutor might have winked or smiled at the jurors, as though they were friends or confidants.

These subtle maneuvers continue into the trial, which begins with opening statements by both the defense and prosecution. The attorneys at this point usually lay out their game plan, stating in no uncertain terms their point of view, the arguments they plan to make, and why they know that their side of the case is just. The attorneys may strut around the courtroom; they may tell jokes; they make speak loudly or softly; they may lean against the rail of the jury box. But all the while, they're also studying the jurors, looking for their reactions, trying to measure how to play the next line or make the next point. As Norman Sheresky explains in his book *On Trial: Masters of the Courtroom*,

> There is a delicate skill involved in communicating with a jury, and the grand master has refined it to a high art form. Instinctively, he is able to convey to them this kind of message: Trust me; I know you, I understand you, I respect you, I like you, and, most important, I will not

mislead you. I know the law, I know what justice is and what it should be. I need your help. Justice depends upon you. Justice is with my client. Your duty is to do justice, as is mine.

At the ideal trial, attorneys on both sides are equally competent at stating their position and impressing the jury with their earnestness and righteousness. The jurors are therefore probably confused: Who is telling the truth? Whom should we believe?

Fortunately, the jurors will have much more to evaluate than merely the lawyers' words. Following the attorneys' opening statements, the heart of the trial begins, during which both sides call witnesses and present physical evidence in an effort to persuade the jury. The prosecution may present a knife that, it claims, is the murder weapon; in rebuttal, the defense may present a medical examiner who says that the victim's wounds are inconsistent with this particular knife.

Foremost in the attorneys' minds during all this are the questions, How does this look to the jury? Are they impressed by what they're seeing? Are they confused?

Because the saying "Seeing is believing" is so often true, attorneys on both sides are very careful about the image that they and their clients project. In a criminal case, for instance, the defendant might be in jail without bail. But because prison clothes might suggest in the minds of jurors that a defendant is already guilty, defendants are allowed to wear normal street clothes. Defense attorneys recommend that male clients wear a suit and tie and female clients a business suit or conservative dress to appear as respectable (and therefore innocent) as possible.

Experience and research have shown that, in the courtroom, appearances do count. Studies have also shown, however, that appearances are often deceiving. Research has found that good-looking defendants tend to be convicted at lower rates, and receive lesser sentences, than defendants who are unattractive. One

Claus von Bulow (right), a New York socialite, listens to testimony during his trial for the attempted murder of his wife, Sunny. Studies indicate that a defendant's appearance and demeanor count with jurors. Defendants who appear sad, for example, are acquitted more often than those who seem happy or angry, and good-looking defendants may have an edge over less attractive ones.

study found that defendants who look sad are more often acquitted than ones who look happy or angry. It has also been found that jurors have a tendency to believe witnesses who seem pleasant and likable, even though researchers have found that likability has no bearing on whether or not a witness is telling the truth.

In *Verdict: The Jury System*, author Morris J. Bloomstein gives an extreme example of how appearances can be deceiving:

> A legendary story that has circulated among lawyers for many years is that of a case in which the defendant was accused of poisoning another person. The balance of the poison, in a bottle, was placed in evidence and rested on the counsel table. The defendant's attorney picked up the bottle, gazed at the jury, and said, "I will show you how certain I am that this is not poison." He then gulped down the contents of the bottle. While the jury, duly impressed, retired and found a verdict of "not guilty," the attorney rushed across the street and had his stomach

A witness testifies at the trial of four reputed mobsters. Researchers have found that juries often judge the credibility of witnesses based on irrelevant factors such as whether the witness was pleasant on the stand.

pumped out. Knowing that it was a slow-acting poison, he had arranged in advance for the medical apparatus to be made ready.

In civil trials, another issue often comes into play: complexity. Some civil cases are so complex, and involve such subtle legal issues, that jurors can make little sense out of what they're hearing. For instance, in a 1978 California trial in which computer giant IBM had been accused of monopolizing a number of computer industry markets, a mistrial had to be declared when the jury couldn't reach a verdict after a five-month trial and three weeks of deliberation. Before declaring the mistrial, the judge called the jurors to his chamber to find out their level of understanding regarding the technologically and financially complicated case. He asked them to define basic terms that were mentioned often at trial, such as *software* and *interface*, but a number of the jurors had no idea what he was talking about.

The problem of complexity has gotten so bad that in 1984, Chief Justice Warren Burger was moved to say, "Even Jefferson would be appalled at the prospect of a dozen of his stout yeomen and artisans trying to cope with some of today's complex litigation."

To forestall such problems, corporations have been known to create mock jury panels to test their trial strategy. In a 1977 case, again involving IBM, the company created a six-person "shadow jury" that followed the trial and discussed their impressions with IBM lawyers daily. With that information, the IBM lawyers had a good idea when the real jury might be getting confused and the next day could adapt their presentation to make their case more understandable to the real jury.

In another case, the telecommunications firm MCI used a mock jury in its suit against rival AT&T. Jury consultants created the mock jury to match the projected makeup of the real jury. They then conducted a mock trial in which MCI specified $100 million in damages for lost profits, after which they watched the mock jury's deliberations through a one-way mirror. The mock jury ultimately granted MCI exactly what the company had asked for. In a second mock trial, MCI offered a nonspecific figure, and the jury came back with a $900 million award. So in the real trial, MCI's attorneys decided not to be specific about damages. The jury decided on $600 million, which, when tripled for punitive purposes, gave MCI $1.8 billion, a record antitrust award.

Making it doubly difficult for jurors to understand a complex case is the prohibition against note taking, which many, but not all, judges enforce because they feel that note taking is an unreliable practice. A juror's notes, these judges fear, might be inaccurate, or a juror might fail to write down something crucial. Some judges also fear that note takers might have undue influence over deliberations.

Evidence from the Simpson trial. Above: Exhibit for the prosecution. Facing page: If the glove doesn't fit, they will acquit. When the jury saw Simpson have trouble putting on the blood-soaked gloves worn by the murderer, the prosecution's case suffered a crippling blow.

Many jurors don't like this restriction—or many of the other rules that judges usually enforce, including a prohibition against discussing the case with anyone, even other jurors, until the deliberations have officially begun. In high-profile cases, jurors are also prohibited from reading newspapers and watching television, and in very rare cases they are actually sequestered during the course of the trial. Such was the case in the criminal trial of O. J. Simpson, when jurors lived in a hotel for 266 days. Because of trial delays, weekends, holidays, and illness, only half of those days were actually spent in court.

When jurors are sequestered, they are allowed only minimal contact with the outside world, including infrequent visits with family and few phone calls. The Simpson jurors, however, were unusual in that they were treated almost like celebrities—they were taken on outings, and famous entertainers, including comedian Jay Leno, actually gave them private performances.

After all the witnesses have testified and all the evidence has been presented, attorneys on both sides of a case present their closing arguments, which are also

called summations. Just as in their opening statements, adept attorneys pull out all the stops, using logic, emotion, and personal appeals to sway the jurors to their side. In the O. J. Simpson criminal case, defense attorney Johnnie Cochran even resorted to rhyme, telling the jury, "If the glove doesn't fit, you must acquit," an allusion to the fact that a bloody glove found on Simpson's property appeared not to fit the defendant when he tried to put it on in front of the jury.

One might assume that after the closing arguments, the courtroom portion of the trial is over, but a crucial element remains: the judge's instructions to the jury. Up to this point, the jury has heard the facts of the case and the arguments presented by both sides. What has been missing is the actual law.

Jurors may know that a defendant is on trial for murder or burglary, but do they know the legal definitions of murder in the second degree, or fourth-degree burglary? The definitions can be quite complex, and it's the judge's job to explain them. The judge also explains a host of other issues. For example, he or she usually tells the jury the steps it must take in making a determination of guilt or innocence, sometimes even providing a checklist of pertinent factors. The judge will usually instruct the jury that the evidence must show the defendant's guilt "beyond a reasonable doubt" and will explain the meaning of this phrase. If a defendant in a criminal case didn't take the stand, the judge may remind jurors of the Fifth Amendment, which states that a person doesn't have to be a witness against himself, and therefore the jury should draw no adverse conclusion from the defendant's decision not to testify.

In a civil case, the judge will explain how damages are to be computed and may also tell the jurors to measure proof not by the number of witnesses but by the quality of their testimony. He or she will define technical terms such as *liability* and will explain that to find the defendant liable, the jury must feel that "a preponderance of the evidence" supports this view—a much lower standard of proof than the criminal trial's "beyond a reasonable doubt."

The judge in either a criminal or civil case may also give the jury brief advice on gauging the credibility of the witnesses who have testified. For example, he or she may advise that jurors take into account the witnesses' demeanor, apparent intelligence, and opportunity to have observed what they described. In addition, the judge may emphasize, the jury should consider whether a particular witness may have a special interest in the outcome of the case and whether there was corroboration of the testimony. The judge may instruct that if jurors believe a witness has lied, they can disregard his or her complete testimony or just the part they believe to be untrue.

Depending on the length and complexity of the case, the judge's instructions—or charge to the jury, as it's sometimes called—may take minutes or days to recite. In rare cases, the judge will give jurors a written copy of his or her instructions; most of the time, the jurors are expected to commit the instructions to memory, although if they forget something or have a question, they can always ask the judge to repeat the instructions or explain in more detail a particular portion.

Once the judge has finished his or her instructions, the end of the courtroom phase of the trial is usually in sight. All the action in the case and all the responsibility is now finally handed to the jurors, who are escorted to a private room where they must grapple with the sometimes overwhelming task of reaching a verdict.

DELIBERATIONS

The witnesses and evidence have been presented. Attorneys for both sides have made their arguments. The judge has instructed the jury. Now the fate of the case is in the jury's hands. It's decision time.

But how, exactly, does a jury reach a decision? There is no easy answer to this question. For one thing, there are no strict guidelines for jurors to follow, no manual they can turn to that will tell them, step by step, what to do. The only action they're required to take is to select, before deliberations begin, a foreperson (although in some courts, the judge has already done

The jurors take a vote in the motion picture 12 Angry Men. *One landmark study found that, notwithstanding the dramatic turnaround depicted in the movie, a jury's first ballot predicts the eventual outcome 90 percent of the time, and rather than being high-minded discussions of the evidence, deliberations are often exercises in badgering and intimidating the minority into going along with the group.*

Before they begin deliberating, jurors are instructed on the relevant law by the trial judge. They don't always follow the judge's instructions, however.

this for them, usually by assigning the task to the first person chosen to serve on the jury). But once that's done, jurors are on their own. And since each jury is composed of a unique combination of individuals—people who were strangers to each other before the trial started—every jury produces its own unique approach, its own way of grappling with the issues at hand.

Another obstacle to understanding what happens inside the jury room is the secrecy that surrounds deliberations. The tradition of secrecy became codified into law after a group of social scientists tried to study the inner workings of the jury room by taping actual deliberations. In 1955, with the permission of the judge and counsel but without the jurors' knowledge, the researchers viewed the deliberations in five civil cases in federal district court in Wichita, Kansas. An uproar ensued when news of the project was leaked, and subsequently Congress and 30 states passed laws prohibiting the taping of deliberations.

During breaks in their deliberations, jurors are not permitted to discuss what has transpired in the jury room with the outside world or even with one another. And often, especially in cases involving serious crimes, jurors are sequestered during deliberations—which means they must stay in a hotel and have little or no contact with the outside world (sequestration is actually mandatory in New York State, regardless of the severity of the crime). Sequestration is based on the old English practice of locking up jurors without food or water to force them to make a rapid verdict; but it also serves the purpose of protecting jurors from outside influences during their deliberations.

Once the trial is over, jurors are free to speak as they please. This is how we have some inkling of what actually transpires behind the closed doors of the jury room. Often attorneys for both sides will quiz the jurors afterward to find out how and why they reached their decision; and in cases being covered by the press, reporters will sometimes go to great lengths to get exclusive interviews with jurors, who then share the sometimes impassioned conflicts and the give-and-take that preceded the final decision.

Often jurors choose to start with an initial ballot in the hope of discovering that they all agree on a verdict (or verdicts, in cases involving multiple charges or claims). Unanimity on the first ballot is rare, but it does happen. In such cases, the jurors' work is complete in a matter of minutes. But when there is disagreement among the jurors, true deliberation begins.

In its ideal form, deliberation consists of a high-minded exchange of ideas. Jurors lay out their views, discuss the evidence in detail, and reason with one another to reach a unanimous (or in some cases, discussed below, a majority) verdict. This form of deliberation is immortalized in the motion picture *12 Angry Men*, in which a lone juror convinces 11 others to change their votes from guilty to not guilty. And yet such dramatic turnarounds are rare in real life, the experts say.

Harry Kalven Jr. and Hans Zeisel, in their landmark 1966 book, *The American Jury*, wrote that deliberations in a vast majority of cases are not significant in changing the minds of jurors. In 90 percent of cases, the majority reflected by the first ballot determines the ultimate verdict, Kalven and Zeisel said. And those in the minority, rather than being persuaded through reason, are often badgered and influenced by peer pressure to change their minds by the anxious majority, who are convinced of their correctness and see no reason to waste time with methodical discussion. But *12 Angry Men* is not a complete fantasy, for Kalven and Zeisel found that in the remaining 10 percent of cases, the jurors who voted in the minority on the first ballot were able to turn around the minds of the majority, producing a verdict opposite what the initial ballot projected.

Researchers have found that, in general, juries take one of two approaches in their deliberations. The first is the verdict-driven deliberation. In this scenario, jurors who voted in the majority identify the jurors who voted in the minority and try to persuade, convince, cajole, or intimidate them into changing their minds. The other scenario is the evidence-driven deliberation, in which jurors do not take an initial vote. Rather, before voting, they carefully review every piece of evidence, and each juror is allowed to speak without interruption. In this way, all the issues are discussed before the jurors take a position.

The juries in the two O. J. Simpson trials adopted different approaches. In the criminal trial, the jury voted right after picking a forewoman. The initial vote was 10 for acquittal and 2 for conviction. The two who favored the guilty verdict then talked about their reservations, and the discussion that followed was geared toward convincing them to change their minds. In less than four hours they had done so, and the jurors returned with a verdict of not guilty in the murders of Nicole Brown Simpson and Ronald Goldman.

In the civil trial, a different jury took a different approach. Rather than take an initial vote, they

Jurors are prohibited from discussing the case until they file into the jury room. After that, however, there are virtually no guidelines for how they may reach a verdict.

The U.S. Supreme Court, 1972. In a decision that year, the Court ruled that states could allow verdicts in noncapital criminal trials by a 9-3 margin. The Court declared that this would not affect the reliability of a verdict because the government would still have proven its case beyond a reasonable doubt to a "super-majority" of jurors. But dissenters Thurgood Marshall (standing, second from left) and William Douglas (seated, second from left) declared that if even one juror objected, the government hadn't adequately proven its case, and Potter Stewart (seated, left) wrote that unanimous verdicts were a safeguard against "community passion and prejudice."

reviewed the trial and the evidence. After discussing the evidence, they found Simpson liable for the deaths of Goldman and Ms. Simpson and ordered him to pay $25 million in punitive damages for both their deaths and $8.5 million in compensatory damages for the death of Goldman. The jury took three days to reach the $8.5 million verdict, and the decision was unanimous (a majority of only 9 out of 12 is required in civil trials in California). The $25 million verdict took them another five hours to decide, and this decision was not unanimous—one juror felt Simpson should not have been held liable at all, while two others felt the amount of the award was excessive.

How could two juries produce such different results? One factor in the Simpson case is the lower standard of proof required to find against a defendant in a civil trial—a preponderance, or majority, of the evidence suffices, whereas proof beyond a reasonable doubt is necessary to convict in a criminal trial. But that aside, juries often produce contradictory—even nonsensical—conclusions.

In the trial of El Sayyid A. Nosair, who was accused of shooting and killing Rabbi Meir Kahane in 1991, a jury acquitted Nosair on the murder charge but found him guilty of possessing the murder weapon. To the public and the prosecution, the verdict made no sense: the jury agreed that Nosair was caught running from the scene of the murder with the murder weapon in his hand, but they didn't think he was guilty of shooting Kahane. Still, regardless of how nonsensical the verdict seemed, it was the final word on the matter.

Not only can a jury render a decision that defies logic, jurors can even render a decision that disregards the judge's instructions and the laws that underlie them. Known as "jury nullification," this has been used historically for both high-minded purposes—in the face of tyrannical laws, for instance—and for despicable ends, such as keeping African Americans "in their place."

During the Vietnam War, protestors who were arrested often relied on jury nullification. In 1973, for example, 28 people went on trial in Camden, New Jersey, for destroying records at the local draft office; they had been caught in the act by Federal Bureau of Investigation agents. The judge allowed the antiwar demonstrators to mount a jury nullification defense.

The defense attorney likened his clients' actions to the Boston Tea Party. "No one would say that breaking into a ship shouldn't be . . . a crime," the attorney argued.

> But in those particular circumstances, would people be convicted of doing that? That's the question. This power that jurors have is the reason why we have you jurors sitting there instead of computers. Because you are supposed to be the conscience of the community. You are supposed to decide if the law, as the judge explains it to you, should be applied or if it should not.

The jury acquitted all the defendants.

Members of Operation Rescue, an antiabortion organization, tried a similar defense in 1990 in San Diego, when they were put on trial for attempting to shut down several abortion and family-planning clinics. The defendants admitted to trespassing but argued that they should be acquitted anyway because it was an act of civil disobedience. The judge, however, denied that the defendants had a right to nullification, and the prosecutor said that the history of jury nullification was tainted—the only time he knew it had been used was when juries in the South said it was acceptable for Ku Klux Klan members to murder blacks. The jurors, regardless of the judge's opposition to jury nullification, could have decided as they pleased once they were in the privacy of the jury room; but they chose to ignore the nullification option, and many of the defendants were convicted.

A jury's decisions are not 100 percent protected against reversal, however. If juror misconduct is uncov-

ered, a higher court can call for a retrial. Such misconduct might range from a juror's accepting a bribe to
communicating improperly with the litigants to lying
about his or her background during the jury-selection
process. Also, if a higher court later finds some other
problem with the trial—that, for instance, the judge
gave faulty instructions—then the jury's verdict can be
erased and a new trial ordered.

Although many people think that jurors must
produce a unanimous vote, in certain cases a "superma-
jority" is all that's required. For instance, civil trials are
not required constitutionally at the state level to have
unanimous verdicts, and 33 states permit nonunanimous verdicts. And in 1972, the Supreme Court found
that states can allow criminal verdicts in noncapital
cases by a 10-2 or even a 9-3 margin.

A majority of justices felt that such a vote wouldn't
change the reliability of the verdict because the case
had still been proved beyond a reasonable doubt to a
large majority of jurors. But other justices felt that
without unanimous verdicts, minority views could be
ignored. Justice Potter Stewart voted in favor of retain-
ing unanimous verdicts. Human behavior is such that
the requirement of unanimity is a necessary "and effective method endorsed by centuries of experience and
history to combat the injuries to the fair administration
of justice that can be inflicted by community passion
and prejudice," Stewart wrote. Justices Thurgood
Marshall and William Douglas said that if one juror
objected, then the government had not proven its case
beyond a reasonable doubt. "Assuming the juror is
mentally competent," they declared, "the 'irrationality'
that enters into the deliberation process is precisely the
essence of the right to a jury trial."

But for Justice Lewis Powell, who favored nonunanimous verdicts, the push for unanimity forced jurors to
compromise, "despite the frequent absence of a rational
basis for such compromise." Ultimately the verdict

reflected "not . . . full agreement among the 12," Powell reasoned, "but . . . agreement by none and compromise by all."

Various states make provisions for nonunanimous verdicts, but usually only in civil cases. Some provide for three-quarters, others five-sixths, others two-thirds majority verdicts. In criminal cases, Idaho allows for verdicts by a five-sixths majority, as does Oregon (except in first-degree murder cases). With crimes less than felonies, Montana permits verdicts by two-thirds majorities; Texas, by three-fourths majorities.

Sometimes a jury simply can't reach a verdict, however. When that happens, it is referred to as a "hung jury." According to *The American Jury*, which was published in 1966, hung juries occurred 5.6 percent of the time in jurisdictions requiring a unanimous verdict and only 3.1 percent of the time in nonunanimous jurisdictions. When a jury initially claims that it can't reach a verdict, the judge often urges the jurors to keep trying, but if a verdict is still not forthcoming, the judge declares a mistrial, and the prosecutor, or the plaintiff, has the option of retrying the case.

In civil trials, jurors sometimes never reach a verdict because both the plaintiff and the defendant, fearing a negative outcome, feel pressure to negotiate a settlement while the jury is deliberating. Also, if a jury reaches a verdict that is extreme—for instance, finding that a minor injury is worth millions of dollars in compensatory damages—a judge may reduce the award.

In capital cases, jurors are often called on make two decisions: whether the defendant is guilty and, if so, whether he or she should be executed. Only after the jury has reached a guilty verdict does the trial move on to the second—penalty—phase. During this phase, the jury hears evidence that may not have been admitted during the first phase of the trial, including, for example, aggravating circumstances such as the defendant's deliberate cruelty, mitigating circumstances such as evidence about the defendant's difficult childhood, and testimony from bereaved friends and relatives of the victim about the impact of the defendant's actions on their lives. Typically, a jury must unanimously agree on a death sentence or the defendant automatically receives life imprisonment.

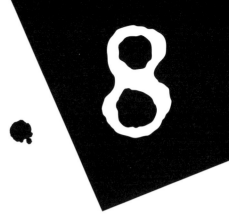

THE VERDICT AND ITS AFTERMATH

"**M**adam Forewoman, has the jury reached a verdict?"

"Yes it has, Your Honor."

With these words, the trial is almost over. The forewoman or foreman passes to the bailiff a piece of paper on which the verdict (or verdicts) is written. The bailiff then hands the paper to the judge, who, after reading the verdict silently, returns the paper to the bailiff, who passes it back to the forewoman or foreman to be read aloud.

Immediately preceding the reading of the verdict, a heavy silence usually falls over the courtroom. This is the moment everyone has been waiting for. But as

The verdict: not guilty. In the time-honored manner, the winning side celebrates the jury's decision—in this case, to acquit Captain Joseph Hazelwood (right) of charges that he was drunk when his ship, the Exxon Valdez, *ran aground in 1989, spilling 11 million gallons of crude oil into Alaska's Prince William Sound.*

soon as the verdict is read, the room usually explodes with noise.

It's a time of great emotion for all concerned. The winning side usually reacts ebulliently by hugging, congratulating each other, and offering thanks, while the losing side is usually dejected, depressed, sometimes even frantic with grief.

The jurors, too, may have strong feelings. Many feel proud for having carried out the task assigned to them. Some are happy that their lives can now return to normal. A few who perhaps changed their minds after much debate may feel frustrated or uneasy as they grapple with lingering doubts.

Generally speaking, the jury's word is final. In certain civil cases, however, the judge may enter judgment *non obstante veredicto,* or notwithstanding the jury's verdict. This overruling of a jury's decision occurs when the jury has ignored a directed verdict—that is, when the judge has ordered the jury to return a certain verdict because, as a matter of law, one party has failed to meet its burden of proof, and the jury fails to do so. In addition, a verdict is sometimes overturned on appeal, but this is usually because of trial errors over which the jury had no control. Once, in a 1992 trial in California, a juror publicly disavowed her guilty verdict in an assault case. She claimed that the other jurors had bullied her and that she never really agreed with the verdict. She went so far as to ask the judge to set aside the verdict, and, in a move that legal experts found surprising, the judge granted her request and ordered a new trial.

For some jurors, the trial doesn't end with the verdict. In horrific cases especially, the stress of the trial can linger, sometimes for weeks or even months. In a study of 40 jurors who had participated in four trials in the Cincinnati area involving killing or sex crimes, 27 (or more than 67 percent) were found to have suffered psychological problems after the trial. Symptoms included sleeplessness, anxiety, stomach-

aches, headaches, heart palpitations, and depression.

After a trial in which a man was found guilty of killing his wife with a homemade spear, one juror was later quoted as saying, "It was frightening to see pictures of her body, with blood everywhere. And we had to look at them over and over again during the trial. Several of us on the jury had nightmares about it." After particularly wrenching trials, judges sometimes arrange for jurors to meet with psychologists or other mental health professionals, who may explain to them possible psychological aftereffects of the trial and who make themselves available if jurors need to talk about their feelings.

Sometimes a verdict itself can have a far-reaching impact on society. Perhaps the most dramatic recent example of this was the verdict issued by a California

Occasionally a jury's verdict has profound effects outside the courtroom. In Los Angeles rioting, looting, and arson followed the 1992 acquittal of four white police officers charged in the beating of Rodney King, a black motorist. Fifty-two people died in the riots, and damage was estimated at nearly $1 billion.

state jury in the case against four white Los Angeles Police Department officers accused of beating Rodney G. King, a black construction worker.

On the night of March 3, 1991, after police attempted to pull his car over for a traffic violation, King led them on a chase at speeds that at times exceeded 100 miles per hour. When he was finally stopped, King initially refused to get out of the car and resisted being handcuffed. But long after it appeared that police had subdued him—while he was on the ground and apparently pleading for mercy—three officers continued to beat King with nightsticks as a sergeant looked on. A man on a nearby balcony captured the entire two-minute beating on videotape, and soon the tape was aired on television stations across the country.

The images were so shocking, and the police use of excessive force seemingly so self-evident, that most people assumed the four officers would be convicted of assault charges at their trial in 1992. But when, on April 29, the white jury from suburban Simi Valley returned verdicts of not guilty, the public's initial surprise quickly gave way to widespread outrage, particularly among African Americans. Angry residents of South Central Los Angeles, a mostly minority neighborhood, took to the streets, and days of rioting and looting ensued. By the time 10,000 police, National Guard officers, and federal troops had restored order four days later, 52 people had been killed, more than 2,000 others had been injured, and nearly 14,000 buildings had been burned, looted, or vandalized. The damage was estimated at almost $1 billion.

The jurors themselves became objects of ridicule and the targets of death threats. "My life is beyond hell," confessed one juror, Alice Debord, to a reporter. Ms. Debord had received death threats shortly after the verdict.

Also much criticized that same year was the state jury that acquitted Lemrick Nelson Jr., a 17-year-old black youth, of fatally stabbing Yankel Rosenbaum, a 29-year-old Hasidic scholar, in the Crown Heights section of Brooklyn in New York City. Among the evidence: Nelson had been arrested near the scene; the alleged murder weapon was in his pocket; police said that Rosenbaum had identified Nelson as his attacker before he died; and Nelson himself had made two confessions.

The not guilty verdict so incensed some people that the New York City Council passed a resolution condemning it, and many people attended protest rallies. The case also figured prominently in the ultimate election defeat of Mayor David Dinkins, who was roundly criticized in some circles for failing to condemn Nelson's acquittal.

Although technically a person found innocent at a trial may not be tried again for the same offense (such a situation is referred to as double jeopardy), the sense that jurors had erred in both the King and Rosenbaum trials was so strong that ultimately pressure was applied to federal prosecutors, who stepped in and charged the defendants in both cases with violating the civil rights of the victims, and in both subsequent trials the defendants were found guilty.

Jurors in high-profile cases sometimes enjoy brief fame. They are interviewed by reporters, appear on talk shows, and sometimes even land a book contract. Several jurors in the criminal trial of O. J. Simpson wrote books, and one, Tracey Hampton, even posed nude in *Playboy*.

But the vast majority of jurors remain nameless to the public at large. They return to their jobs, families, and lives with firsthand knowledge of how the criminal justice system works and, perhaps, with a sense of satisfaction regarding their contributions to justice.

CAN THE JURY SYSTEM BE IMPROVED?

The jury system has withstood the test of time—but not without considerable changes. Once, jurors with personal knowledge of the case were preferred; today, such knowledge is a bar to service. In the past, vast segments of the population were excluded from serving; today, many safeguards are in place to help ensure that a cross section of society is reflected on juries. Also, the sizes of today's juries sometimes vary, and verdicts need no longer always be unanimous.

Still, calls for additional changes are periodically

Los Angeles district attorney Gil Garcetti (right) and two prosecutors at a press conference following the first murder trials of Lyle and Erik Menendez. When the juries hearing both cases failed to reach a verdict, mistrials were declared. Critics felt that the evidence against the two brothers, charged with murdering their wealthy parents in their Beverly Hills home, had been so overwhelming that the hung juries pointed to a flaw in the jury system, and some Californians called for allowing nonunanimous verdicts in murder cases.

voiced. These calls invariably follow high-profile cases in which much of the public disagrees with the jury's verdict. For instance, in the first trials of Lyle and Eric Menendez, who were accused of killing their wealthy parents with shotguns in their Beverly Hills home, the juries hearing each of their cases couldn't reach unanimous verdicts, and mistrials were declared for both defendants. The brothers' attorneys had mounted an abuse defense—admitting that their clients had killed their parents but attributing their actions to years of physical, sexual, and psychological abuse. To many in the public and the media, these claims didn't ring true. The brothers, they believed, were spoiled rich kids who had murdered their parents to get a large inheritance, initially trying to make the crime appear as if it had been committed by someone else, and only after being caught had they concocted the abuse story. Any trial outcome less than guilty verdicts, many of these critics argued, pointed to faults in the jury system. Indeed, the Menendez mistrials provoked much discussion about allowing nonunanimous verdicts in such cases in California, although the law was never changed in that regard. (The brothers were subsequently convicted at another, joint trial.)

Another recent, famous case also produced cynicism about the jury system. That case involved a white mob in the Bensonhurst neighborhood of Brooklyn, New York, that beat, shot, and killed Yusuf Hawkins, a young black man. Joseph Fama and Keith Mondello were tried together, but two separate juries considered their fates. Fama was convicted of murder, but Mondello, who confessed to having led the gang, was acquitted. As Stephen J. Adler explains in *The Jury: Trial and Error in the American Courtroom*, "The split verdicts simply didn't make sense, and in the avalanche of newspaper columns and street demonstrations that followed, the jury system came across as an awfully feeble force for criminal justice and racial healing."

Although much has been done to reform the way prospective jurors are selected, opening the pool to a larger range of the population representing both sexes and all races and economic backgrounds, many feel that still more could be done to open the jury box further during the voir dire. In particular, many feel that peremptory challenges allow attorneys secretly to cull from the jury just those people earlier reforms were intended to include. Supreme Court justice Thurgood Marshall wrote in a 1986 decision that the Court should "ideally" ban peremptory challenges altogether because of the "inherent potential of peremptory challenges to distort the jury process by permitting the exclusion of jurors on racial grounds."

Although the Supreme Court has outlawed challenges based on sex and race, it hasn't gone as far as the British Parliament, which in 1988 banned peremptory challenges completely. As a result, jury selection in Great Britain proceeds much more quickly. In Britain, usually only 20 prospective jurors are culled randomly from voter lists for a criminal trial, then 12 are randomly selected. Lawyers may not even ask them questions, but may merely look them over for visual clues that a juror has a conflict of interest and challenge him or her for cause. The process takes only minutes as opposed to the days it often takes in the United States.

Another reform some have called for are rules making the judge's instructions more comprehensible. This is especially relevant in civil trials, in which the laws governing a particular dispute are sometimes so complex and arcane that even the judge has trouble understanding them. Often the judge's main concern is that

Keith Mondello (above) and Joseph Fama were members of a white mob that killed a black youth in Brooklyn's Bensonhurst neighborhood. Mondello and Fama were tried together but had separate juries, and although Mondello admitted leading the mob, his jury found him not guilty; Fama's jury, on the other hand, convicted him of murder. To many observers the split verdicts made no sense.

the instructions be fair and complete, so as to prevent the jury's ultimate decision from being overturned on appeal. And yet the criteria of fairness and completeness sometimes have no bearing on whether jurors of average intelligence and experience can understand what the judge is saying. As Judge Jerome Frank, a federal jurist, said in 1949, jurors have "infinite capacity for mischief, for 12 men can easily misunderstand more law in a minute than a judge can explain in an hour."

"Terms such as *liability, damages, inference, execute, representation, immaterial, preponderance of the evidence, admissibility*, and *burden of proof*, which seem self-evident to lawyers, baffle jurors," Stephen Adler writes. "Instructions are thick with complex, multiclause sentences, passive constructions, and multiple negatives." Because of this, some have even called for a "complexity exception" to the Seventh Amendment right to a jury trial in civil cases. This would allow the judge to decide a case without a jury if he or she thinks the jury wouldn't be able to understand the law. At this point, however, the so-called complexity exception remains just the dream of a few legal reformers.

One thing judges might do to help jurors grapple with a case is to read their instructions at the beginning of the trial rather than after all the witnesses and evidence have been presented. That way, jurors would have a key to help them decipher the arguments and could be on the lookout for important information that would help them reach a verdict. Some judges, in fact, do this already, but most wait until the end of the trial, in part because they need to see the trial before they know exactly which instructions are most appropriate.

Perhaps one of the most significant criticisms lobbed at jurors in recent years is that they are inclined to grant terrifically large awards in civil trials. Business interests have been particularly upset by these awards because they feel that jurors are too willing to side with individual plaintiffs against large, anonymous corporations. Juries also sometimes make capricious judgments, basing their decisions on arbitrary factors. For example, in the $10.5 billion award for Pennzoil against Texaco in 1986, jurors admitted afterward that they added $1 billion to the award for every witness for Texaco to whom they took a strong dislike. (The parties eventually settled for $3 billion.)

Vice President Dan Quayle made the reform of civil lawsuits (called tort reform) an issue in the 1992 presidential campaign. Quayle claimed that the wasted cost of the jury-based civil liability system was nearly $300 billion every year, although others have said it's much less, perhaps $130 billion. The Bush administration wanted a $250,000 cap on what juries could award individuals for pain and suffering in medical malpractice suits and also wanted to deny juries the power to set punitive damages (which are damages intended to punish the defendant, not fairly compensate the plaintiff for harm done). The proposals went nowhere on the federal level, but at least 20 states have passed related laws in some form.

In general, however, most civil awards aren't very high, the median being somewhere between $20,000 and $30,000 in all verdicts, including ones against corporations, studies done in the 1980s showed. Some observers have suggested that it would be enough merely to educate jurors more about how to assess damage awards. They could, for instance, be told of past verdicts reached in similar cases, or laws could be put in place that would assign a range of allowable awards for various injuries. Great Britain has handled the situation by gradually reducing the role of juries in civil disputes, so that today English juries hear very few such cases.

Some have suggested that jurors could do a better job if they were allowed at all trials to take notes (currently jurors in a little more than a third of cases are allowed to do this, at the judge's discretion) and even to ask questions of witnesses. In very rare instances,

Vice President Dan Quayle made the reform of civil lawsuits an issue in the 1992 presidential campaign. Quayle decried what he considered excessive awards for "pain and suffering" in medical malpractice cases and punitive damages in product liability cases because, he said, they cost the U.S. economy billions of dollars annually. Others have sought to curtail the jury's role in civil litigation because they feel the legal issues are often too complex for ordinary citizens to grasp.

some judges allow jurors to write down questions and pass them along to the judge, but in most cases jurors are passive receivers of information.

Regardless of what the future brings, however, it's likely that the jury system in the United States will remain in place for a long time. The notion of average citizens making key, sometimes life-and-death decisions is such an integral part of our criminal justice system that the jury's role may never be substantially curtailed.

Perhaps the best way to assess the value of the jury system is to speak to an actual juror. For many jurors, the experience is boring, sometimes confusing, and not a little bit frustrating. Others, however, find jury service eye-opening, enlightening, and memorable.

"I sort of went in consciously saying to myself, 'I don't feel comfortable doing this and I'm afraid of doing it, but I'll see what happens,' " said Michael Thibodeau, a 32-year-old art director who served on a jury in a 1997 Brooklyn murder trial.

Thibodeau said he was initially mistrustful of the criminal justice system and of his fellow jurors. "I was worried that I wouldn't be able to make an informed decision. What if they didn't give me enough information to make a decision? It wasn't that I would be afraid to say guilty or not guilty. I thought it would come to either/or and I would have to flip a coin."

But after 5 days of jury selection and 13 days of trial, Thibodeau felt that he had, in fact, heard enough to say the defendant was guilty of shooting and killing a man outside a party. The jurors reviewed the evidence before taking a first vote, which resulted in a 9-3 tally in favor of conviction. Deliberations carried over to a second day. After much discussion, the three holdouts changed their minds and voted to convict.

Thibodeau says he adhered strictly to the judge's order that the jurors not discuss the trial with anyone outside of the jury room. But he noticed that some of his fellow jurors violated that rule by talking about the case over lunch. He also found some of the personalities of the other jurors annoying, and he thought that they too often veered from the evidence into pure speculation during deliberations.

And yet, despite all that—and almost to his surprise—he concluded that the system worked.

"I guess it worked because we came to a decision. I think one of the good parts of it is, the onus isn't just on you. The burden is on 12 people on the jury. In a lot of ways, it's about building a consensus. It's not letting one person reach a decision. We worked together. And it was organized in the way it moved. There were a couple of battles, and some heavy talk, but we got through it together."

Does he feel the jury ultimately arrived at the truth?

"Only God knows," Thibodeau said. "Nobody else was there besides the person who was shot . . . [but] judging from the testimony and physical evidence, I think [we] made the right decision."

Further Reading

Abramson, Jeffrey. *We, the Jury.* New York: Basic Books, 1994.

Adler, Stephen J. *The Jury: Trial and Error in the American Courtroom.* New York: Time Books, 1994.

Bloomstein, Morris J. *Verdict: The Jury System.* New York: Dodd, Mead, 1972.

Kalven, Harry, Jr., and Hans Zeisel. *The American Jury.* Reprint. Chicago: University of Chicago Press, 1986.

Kolanda, Jo, and Judge Patricia Curley. *Trial by Jury.* New York: Franklin Watts, 1988.

Sheresky, Norman. *On Trial: Masters of the Courtroom.* New York: Viking Press, 1977.

Thornton, Hazel. *Hung Jury: The Diary of a Menendez Juror.* Philadelphia: Temple University Press, 1995.

Van Dyke, Jon M. *Jury Selection Procedures: Our Uncertain Commitment to Representative Panels.* Cambridge, Mass.: Ballinger Publishing Co., 1977.

Williams, Mary E., ed. *The Jury System.* San Diego: Greenhaven Press, 1997.

Wishman, Seymour. *Anatomy of a Jury: The System on Trial.* New York: Times Books, 1986.

Zerman, Melvyn Bernard. *Beyond a Reasonable Doubt: Inside the American Jury System.* New York: Crowell, 1981.

ROBERT V. WOLF is a graduate of Columbia University. He is an editor at a daily newspaper in New York City and a freelance writer whose work has appeared in newspapers and magazines around the country. He is also the author of *Capital Punishment* in Chelsea House's Crime, Justice, and Punishment series.

AUSTIN SARAT is William Nelson Cromwell Professor of Jurisprudence & Political Science at Amherst College, where he also chairs the Department of Law, Jurisprudence and Social Thought. Professor Sarat is the author or editor of 23 books and numerous scholarly articles. Among his books are *Law's Violence, Sitting in Judgment: Sentencing the White Collar Criminal*, and *Justice and Injustice in Law and Legal Theory*. He has received many academic awards and held several prestigious fellowships. In addition, he is a nationally recognized teacher and educator whose teaching has been featured in the *New York Times*, on the *Today* show, and on National Public Radio's *Fresh Air*.

Picture Credits